Monetary and Banking Reform in Postcommunist Economies

A Special Report
edited by
David M. Kemme
and Andrzej Rudka

A compendium of papers presented at the
Institute for East-West Security Studies
conference on
Money, Banking and Credit
in Eastern Europe and the Soviet Union

co-hosted by
the Mitsui Marine Research Institute
and the Japan Center for International Finance
May 15–18, 1991
Tokyo

with an additional chapter by Andrzej Rudka

INSTITUTE FOR EAST-WEST SECURITY STUDIES
NEWYORK·PRAGUE

The Institute for East-West Security Studies does not take or
encourage specific policy positions. It is committed to encouraging and facilitating the discussion of important issues of concern
to East and West. The views expressed in this report do not
necessarily reflect the opinions of the Board of Directors, the
officers, or the staff of the Institute.

Distributed by Westview Press
            5500 Central Avenue
            Boulder, Colorado 80301
            (800) 456-1995

Library of Congress Cataloging-in-Publication data

Monetary and banking reform in postcommunist economies / edited by
David M. Kemme and Andrzej Rudka.
        p.   cm.—(Special report)
    "A compendium of papers presented at the Institute for East-West
Security Studies conference on Money, Banking, and Credit in Eastern
Europe and the Soviet Union, co-hosted by the Mitsui Marine Research
Institute and the Japan Center for International Finance, May 15–18, 1991,
Tokyo."
    Includes bibliographical references.
    ISBN 0-913449-29-6 (IEWSS):$19.85.—ISBN 0-8133-8572-5
(Westview):$19.85
    1. Monetary policy—Europe, Eastern—Congresses. 2. Monetary
policy—Soviet Union—Congresses.   3. Banks and banking—Europe,
Eastern—Congresses.   4. Banks and banking—Soviet Union—
Congresses.   5. Post-communism—Europe, Eastern—Congresses.
6. Post-communism—Soviet Union—Congresses.   I. Kemme, David
M. II. Rudka, Andrzej, 1953–   .   III. Institute for East-West Security
Studies.   IV. Mitsui Marine Research Institute.   V. Kokusai Kin'yū Jōhō
Sentā (Japan)   VI. Series: Special report (Institute for East–West Security
Studies)
    HG930.7.M66   1992   92-827
                                                          CIP

CONTENTS

FOREWORD

Credit and capital are critical lubricants of the mechanisms collectively known as "the market economy"; their most efficient allocation occurs through sophisticated monetary and banking systems that today have global reach. The relatively primitive financial machinery that supported the centrally planned economies of Eastern Europe and the former Soviet Union could not prevent the ultimate failure of communism in the region, and it is clearly ill-suited to the rigors of the transition to and eventual arrival of the free market.

The monetary and banking systems of Eastern Europe and the former Soviet Union require thorough-going reform. Western models have proven instructive, although neither universally nor uniformly. The US, Japanese, and West European systems developed individually, in response to circumstances of history and tradition; no single one of them is completely applicable to the needs of the countries of Eastern Europe or the newly independent republics of the Commonwealth of Independent States. An ideal prescription under such circumstances would include a long period of time for study and experimentation, but such time is not available. The states of the region must act soon, or the unanchored economic "gains" of the last two years could slip away.

In May 1991 the Institute for East-West Security Studies convened a conference on Money, Banking and Credit in Eastern Europe and the Soviet Union. At the conference, held in Tokyo with the collaboration of the Mitsui Marine Research Institute and the Japan Center for International Finance, bankers and financial experts from Poland, Hungary, the Czech and Slovak Federal Republic, the Soviet Union, Bulgaria, and Romania presented reports on the status of banking reform in their countries. Counterparts from Western Europe, Japan, and the United States responded to the presentations with critical analyses and recommendations. The papers presented in this Special Report include selected presentations and a summation of the conference proceedings.

The Institute for East-West Security Studies would like to thank our co-hosts of this important meeting, the Japan Center for International Finance and the Mitsui Marine Research Institute. We are also extremely grateful to the Japan Economic Foundation for its sponsorship of the meeting, and to the Sasakawa Peace Foundation for making this publication possible and for its sponsorship of the Institute's new Banking and Finance Assistance Center in Prague. Thanks are also due to the Pew Charitable Trusts for their ongoing support of the IEWSS Economics Program. In addition, the Institute would like to express gratitude for the support and participation of Mr. Taro Nakayama, then the Minister for Foreign Affairs, and Mr. Michio Watanabe, currently the Deputy Prime Minister and Minister for Foreign Affairs.

John Edwin Mroz
President
Institute for East-West Security
  Studies

Anthony M. Solomon
Chairman
IEWSS Economics Program

January 1992

EDITORS' ACKNOWLEDGMENTS

It was a great pleasure for me to chair the IEWSS conference on "Money, Banking and Credit in Eastern Europe and the Soviet Union." There were a number of individuals critical to the success of the conference and the publication of this Special Report whom I would like to thank. First, with respect to the organization of the conference, David Youtz, IEWSS Coordinator of Asian Programs, Keith Wind, IEWSS Director of Conferences and Special Projects, and IEWSS staff members Rosemarie Roqué and Orin Kurland deserve special thanks. Our counterpart hosts in Japan, the Mitsui Marine Research Institute (MMR) and the Japan Center for International Finance (JCIF) provided excellent guidance and assistance in the planning and execution stages of the conference. In particular I would like to thank Mr. Ichiro Uchida, then of MMR, for his personal encouragement and support and his help in arranging financial support for the conference. His colleagues and the staff at MMR provided invaluable assistance in Tokyo; without them the conference would not have been possible.

With respect to preparing the conference papers for publication, Andrzej Rudka and I would like to thank Rosalie Morales Kearns at the IEWSS and Craig Pospisil at the Barton School of Business, Wichita State University, for their work in copy editing the final manuscript, and Richard Levitt for supervising its production.

Finally, I would like to thank all my colleagues at the Institute for East-West Security Studies for the support, encouragement, collegiality, and intellectual stimulation they provided while I served as Pew Charitable Trusts Economics Scholar-in-Residence during 1989–1991.

David M. Kemme
W. Frank Barton Faculty Fellow
Wichita State University

1

Introduction: An Overview of Monetary and Banking Reform

DAVID M. KEMME
REI MASUNAGA

The allocation of credit and capital in the formerly centrally planned economies of Eastern Europe and the Soviet Union was directly in accordance with annual and five-year physical plans constructed by the national planning commissions. There was no market for financial capital, and liquidity was provided by the national banks via a mechanistic process of direct allocation to enterprises designated in the plans. In a market economy, however, money and capital markets are critical to the efficient allocation of capital and the smooth functioning of the economy. How, in this period of transition from plan to market, will economic policy makers in Eastern Europe and the Soviet Union create a smoothly operating market for money and capital? While the popular press has focused on the creation of stock exchanges in each country, it is the central and commercial banking system that forms the principal institutional structure necessary for the allocation of money and capital. Many critical questions must be analyzed: How are government authorities approaching the need to develop functioning commercial banks and an independent central bank from the existing monobank system? What will happen to existing assets and liabilities of the national banks? What mechanisms will be employed during the transition period to supply liquidity and conduct monetary policy?

Recognizing the importance of these questions and the numerous approaches to their resolution, the Institute for East-

David M. Kemme, formerly the IEWSS Pew Economics Scholar-in-Residence, is the W. Frank Barton Faculty Fellow at the Wichita State University. Rei Masunaga is Deputy President of the Japan Center for International Finance.

1

West Security Studies, in cooperation with the Mitsui Marine Research Institute and the Japan Center for International Finance, sponsored a conference on "Money, Banking and Credit in Eastern Europe and the Soviet Union" held in Tokyo on May 15–18, 1991. Officials from the national banks and ministries of finance of Hungary, Poland, the Czech and Slovak Federal Republic, Bulgaria, Romania, and the USSR met with prominent Western banking and finance practitioners, government officials, and academics. The papers collected in this compendium served as the basis for discussions at the conference and were later revised for this publication. They present an illuminating snapshot of legal, institutional, and financial changes taking place in Eastern Europe and the Soviet Union during this period of rapid change. It is quite evident that each country faces similar problems, but the severity of these problems differs significantly from country to country. Thus, as the following papers indicate, the approaches by policy makers also vary. We will summarize here the common elements of change to date.

In each country the first steps toward creation of a viable banking system have been taken. The monobank system, in which the national bank served as a central bank and a monopolistic commercial bank with a nationwide branch network, has been dismantled. In each country a portion of the assets and liabilities of the national bank were spun off to several newly created state-owned commercial banks. A two-tier banking system has been created, in which the national bank functions as a traditional central bank and the newly created commercial banks, although state-owned, have begun functioning on a profit-oriented basis. However, numerous problems have quickly emerged, several of which were addressed by the conference participants and the authors of the papers presented. First, do the national banks have the necessary independence from the government to conduct effective monetary policy? Second, do the national banks have the requisite instruments to control the money supply and ensure a sufficient and unbiased allocation of aggregate liquidity? Third, is the system of bank oversight and regulation sufficiently developed to monitor bank activity to ensure both sound lending on the one hand and safety of deposits on the other? Fourth, are the newly created commercial banks able to operate as true commercial banks, or are they trapped by the potential losses of the very low-quality assets represented by the loan portfolios inherited from the national bank?

In each country the national banks are indeed at least nominally independent of the government. Each of the papers in this compendium recognizes the need for central bank independence and emphasizes the need for price stability—a principal goal of the central bank in a market economy. The transition period, however, is fraught with policy disputes, and policy debate is intensely politicized. Macro-policy in each country varies, but incipient inflationary pressures exist as weak legislatures pressure the national banks to finance government deficits. The attitudes of the banks vary from the cooperative spirit of the National Bank of the CSFR, where inflationary tendencies were initially relatively small, to the more problematic relationship between the National Bank of Poland and the Ministry of Finance during the early stages of Poland's stabilization program.

In regard to monetary instruments and the ability of the central bank to conduct monetary policy, the traditional instruments utilized in market economies are being developed. Reserve requirements, limited open market operations in the form of intermediation on the market for treasury bills in Hungary and Poland, and discounts or refinancing of enterprise loans made by the commercial banks are the principal instruments for influencing liquidity. As the authors point out, however, the interbank money markets and markets for treasury securities are very thin, where they exist at all. The principal means of regulating the supply of liquidity remains rationing and direct allocation of bank credit, even in Hungary, which has the most developed money and capital market mechanisms.

As the commercial banking industry develops, it is crucial to have in place a system of bank supervision, regulation, and oversight. Again, in each country an appropriate supervisory office has been established. This office may be independent of the central bank—in Hungary it is part of the Ministry of Finance—or it may be a part of the central bank, as in Poland. Regardless of the affiliation of the regulatory agency, the system of bank reporting must provide accurate and up-to-date information to the regulatory authorities, policy makers at the central bank, and the managers of the commercial banks and the central bank. In each country, appropriate steps are being taken to establish an autonomous regulatory and supervisory agency empowered to conduct on-site audits of commercial banks and impose appropriate sanctions. However, the accounting and reporting systems are not yet sufficiently developed to ensure timely and efficient reporting for the purpose of monetary control.

The commercial banks created from the old national banks still dominate the marketplace in terms of share of deposits and share of credit issued. Newly established private banks are typically small, in terms of assets, but have the advantage of clean balance sheets. The assets transferred from the national bank to the newly created banks included a large number of loans of dubious value to state-owned enterprises. Only in the CSFR was there an attempt to shield the newly formed banks from some portion of these poor quality loans. The so-called perpetual loans, which were in effect capital grants to state-owned enterprises, were transferred to the newly created Consolidation Bank. The commercial banks that were spun off the Czechoslovak National Bank were thus free from these troublesome assets. However, as in the other countries of Eastern Europe, the new state-owned commercial banks in the CSFR will undoubtedly face difficulties, as a significant portion of loans has been made to enterprises that are experiencing financial difficulty during the transition.

In Hungary, Poland, Bulgaria, and Romania, the potentially problematic loans were transferred to the new commercial banks. The extent to which these loans should be written off is an open question in both countries, but in any event the rapid inflation in Poland, and to a lesser extent in Bulgaria, has substantially eroded the real value of these assets. Hungary and Bulgaria are also faced with a second problem. The state savings bank is burdened with a large portfolio of low-interest housing loans. Both nonperforming loans to enterprises and low-interest loans to households will reduce earnings in the banking sector and slow growth and innovation in this critical area.

The countries of Eastern Europe are making tremendous strides in bank reform and the creation of viable financial markets. The lessons of reform already learned, many of which are presented in the following papers, are certainly valuable for the former Soviet Union and the anticipated reforms at the republic level. While Gosbank undergoes a transition in and of itself, the new central banks and the commercial banking systems likely to be developed in the new nations formed from the former Soviet republics will be faced with very similar problems. The papers presented here represent a valuable contribution to the accumulation of knowledge and practical experience in economic transition in Eastern Europe and the former Soviet Union. As Tadaie Yamashita concludes in the last essay of this compendium, the policy makers in Eastern Europe and the former Soviet Union are to be commended for the tremendous progress made in such a short time, but this fascinating transition is just beginning.

2

The Transformation and Development of the Hungarian Banking System

AKOS BALASSA

I. Banking Reform and the Development of the Banking System: 1987–1990

A. The Banking System Before 1987

Until the end of 1947, the Hungarian banking system corresponded to the typical European banking system. In addition to the National Bank of Hungary (NBH), founded in 1924, there were a number of merchant banks (including four or five major ones) and many savings banks. Foreign capital played a significant role in the banks. At the end of 1947, the National Bank of Hungary and later all the merchant banks were nationalized. In 1967, the state acquired the shares of foreign shareholders.

In 1948, the Hungarian banking system was transformed in accordance with the Soviet pattern. The National Bank of Hungary performed the tasks of the issuing central bank. It kept the accounts of state enterprises and provided them with loans after the actual closing of the merchant banks (i.e., it also functioned as a commercial bank). Moreover, it enjoyed a virtual monopoly as far as its commercial banking activities were concerned. (Although a few financial institutions were formally maintained, they functioned under the direct control of the NBH, essentially as its branches.) Until 1971, investment loans were provided by the Hungarian Investment Bank, but then the NBH took over these functions as well. In addition, the National Savings Bank provided retail banking services and dealt with the financial

Akos Balassa is Managing Director of the National Bank of Hungary.

transactions of the local councils. The Hungarian Foreign Trade Bank financed foreign trade.

Despite the changes carried out in the banking system since 1948, its major characteristics remained constant throughout. Among these characteristics were the monopoly position enjoyed by the NBH and the lack of competition among banks; the subordination of banking transactions and lending to state decisions within the framework of the national economic plan (e.g., lending not on the basis of business considerations but in line with quantitative plan decisions); the state and bureaucratic nature of banking activities; and the possibility granted to the NBH to interfere in enterprise management and its related controlling functions. All of this took place under conditions where money did not play an active role in the economy; goods and incomes were distributed by the state, and money and capital markets practically did not exist.

In 1968, Hungary began a program of economic reform. The reform abolished the planned economy according to the Soviet model, particularly the determination of mandatory plan targets for enterprises by state organs, and the central distribution of resources in kind. The objective was to develop a model in which the economy would function on the basis of state plans, but the state would not directly control the enterprises. Instead, the state would regulate the market and the conditions of running the enterprises, mainly through the budget and the banking system.

This endeavor, aimed at a combination of the plan and the market, also embraced the idea that the significance and role of the banking system would increase in the economy-controlling activities of the state and in business life. Initially, it was thought that the banking system would be able to perform this task only if the monopoly position of the NBH was maintained. It was expected that the second stage of reform could be introduced about three to five years after the 1968 reform, with measures including the transformation of the banking system and the founding of independent commercial banks.

After the failure of the Prague Spring, however, the external as well as the internal political situation changed radically. The political pressure exerted by the leaders of the Soviet Union and other East European states encouraged and strengthened the Hungarian "conservatives" and weakened the supporters of reform. The second stage of the reform could not be prepared, let alone implemented; in fact, its evolution was halted until the end of the 1970s, and there were even reversals on several points. Thus the transformation of the banking system was struck off the agenda for a long time.

The issue of economic reform was again put forward in the first half of the 1980s, particularly after Hungary's accession to the International Monetary Fund and the World Bank in 1982. The concept behind the 1982–1984 reform returned, in part, to the basic ideas of the 1968 reform and additionally contained proposals for the transformation of the economy in line with the current situation. The objective was to bring the Hungarian economic system closer to that of a market economy. Nevertheless, a full break with the planned economy, employing indirect methods of control, did not take place; nor was the need for a comprehensive reform of ownership acknowledged. The reform process that had begun in 1985 intended to implement the postponed second stage of the 1968 reform, but the concept behind the reform significantly superseded its predecessor on several points (particularly on the issues of monetary control and the establishment of a capital market). The political leadership at the time intended to introduce this second reform on a gradual basis over a period of four or five years. (It was only at the beginning of 1989 that the Hungarian leadership realized the need for a full break with the planned economy and for the transition to a "pure" market economy.)

The transformation of the banking system constituted an organic and extremely important part of the reform process. Certain minor steps had already been taken in the early and mid-1980s. A few specialized financial institutions were formed, primarily to perform investment and innovation functions. The first seeds of interbank competition also appeared as a result. Furthermore, the first banks operating with foreign capital (CIB in 1980, Citibank in 1986, Unicbank in 1987) were established. A radical, comprehensive reform of the banking system was introduced on January 1, 1987. Essentially, the reform was implemented in a single step, even though certain elements were postponed to mid-1987 and then to 1988–1989.

B. The Banking Reform of 1987 and the Banking System's Development Through 1990

The primary purpose of the banking reform of 1987 was to replace the single-tier banking system, namely, the activities of the National Bank of Hungary, which since 1948 had performed both central and commercial banking functions, with a two-tier banking system. In this system monetary policy could function efficiently and market relationships between merchant banks and enterprises free of state intervention could develop.

The function of the National Bank of Hungary changed fundamentally: most of its commercial banking operations were terminated. Since 1987, the NBH has not kept accounts for enterprises nor does it lend to them. The NBH has turned into a real bank of issue. Its primary task is monetary control, that is, issuing money and regulating the money supply and financial transactions. In addition, the NBH serves as bank of the state and of the banks by keeping the accounts of the budget, the central extra-budgetary funds, the central budgetary institutions (from 1987 to the present), and the commercial banks. In 1987, the NBH still retained its foreign exchange banking functions.

The close linkage between the activities of the NBH and the annual national economic plans (still existing then, though abolished in 1990) was terminated in 1987. At the same time, monetary policy continued to be determined by the government, based on recommendations of the president of the National Bank of Hungary. The NBH shifted from determining so-called credit quotas and interest rates on different types of loan facilities to controlling the money supply. It did this primarily through the allocation of refinancing loans to commercial banks and the determination of reserve requirements, and later through open market operations. The NBH applied an interest policy that approximated market rates for refinancing loans; thus it also influenced the interest rates charged by commercial banks freely in accordance with the market situation.

With the reform of 1987, independent commercial banks came into being. Some of them were formed out of the sectoral departments of the NBH. As a result of the reform, they became fully independent from the NBH. In 1987, 21 financial institutions were in operation, five of which were universal commercial banks. The number of financial institutions increased to 28 by the end of 1989 and to 33 by the end of 1990. Three of the generally licensed banks were particularly large, concentrating the decisive part of enterprise accounts. One of the basic principles of the banking system reform was to create banks that would compete against each other. For that purpose, no administrative sectoral or regional specialization or constraint was introduced.

Prior to 1987, enterprises and cooperatives were mandatorily assigned to a particular bank. In the summer of 1987, this mandatory allocation was abolished and the enterprises were granted the right to freely choose their bank. This marked the beginning of competition among banks. Enterprises were entitled to break relations with the bank that could not meet their requirements and turn to others. At first, an enterprise was permitted to have only one bank to keep its current account, although enterprises could borrow from any bank. Since 1989, enterprises have been permitted to have current accounts kept by several banks.

The experience of early 1987 revealed that most industrial enterprises had accounts with the largest bank (Hungarian Credit Bank); the majority of agro-industrial enterprises and cooperatives turned to the second largest bank (National Commercial and Credit Bank); while most of those engaged in infrastructural activities or in the energy sector, to the third largest bank (Budapest Bank). Although the constraints were abolished and a number of enterprises changed banks, the clienteles of the three largest banks continued to exhibit the above profiles, but to a much lesser extent. The smaller and newly established banks found their clients mainly among smaller-scale and new undertakings. Nevertheless, there is a tendency for enterprises that keep their accounts with one of the large banks to also have accounts with the smaller banks and to also borrow from them. The converse is also true: many of the new ventures are among the clients of the large banks.

A somewhat peculiar situation evolved in the areas of retail banking and foreign exchange operations over the last few years. Although commercial banks were licensed to collect deposits from and grant loans to households from the outset, they adopted a policy of "self-restraint" with respect to these activities for a transitional period. Earlier, retail banking had been the exclusive territory of the National Savings Bank (which has since been transformed and provides universal banking services) and of the saving cooperatives. In 1988 the commercial banks began to collect savings of households, in the form of securities, rather than of deposits. (This was related to the specific situation that developed in the area of housing loans.) The Postabank (Post Bank) was established in 1989 primarily to serve households, and has been vigorously developing ever since.

In 1987, the NBH still retained all its foreign exchange banking functions. Since 1989, the export-import deals of enterprises have been administered through the commercial banks (except for contracts payable in transferable rubles, which were kept by the NBH till the end of 1990), but enterprises were required to sell the foreign exchange they earned to the banks and the banks to the NBH. They could buy foreign exchange only from the NBH. Until the end of 1990, commercial banks were permitted to perform foreign exchange lending operations only after obtaining licenses. It should also be noted that enterprises have been able to grant commercial loans and to issue drafts to one another since 1983.

C. The Operation of the Banking System: 1987–1990

The transformation of the banking system in 1987 took place when the comprehensive reform of the entire economy was in its initial phase. Nevertheless, the efficiencies of the two-tier banking system were soon evident, and the system served as a stimulus to continuing reforms and provided favorable conditions for them.

The relationship between enterprises and banks underwent a radical change in the first years of the banking reform. Enterprises interacted not with the organs of the state, but with financial institutions functioning on a business basis following economic objectives only. The relationship between bank and enterprise developed into that of partners on an equal footing. With the increase in the number of banks, competition became keener, which forced banks to develop their services and products. This necessitated the training of thousands of bankers.

The activities of the National Bank of Hungary also changed significantly. Naturally, after the reform the NBH did not (could not) interfere in the activities of the individual banks, nor did it instruct the banks to grant or refuse loans (as it had earlier). Instead of allocating credit lines, the NBH shifted to employing modern instruments of monetary policy. This, however, unfolded only gradually: for several years, the normative nature of monetary control was only partially implemented and, at times, special appraisals and methods were also used.

The transformed banking system faced a number of difficulties in the course of its operation. The banking reform was introduced just after a period of monetary surplus (1985–1986); equilibrium (balance of payments and the government budget) was deteriorating significantly, due in part to the excessive money supply. This deterioration was also linked to the structural problems of the economy: significant amounts were lent to unprofitable enterprises (e.g., mining, iron metallurgy, and agriculture; these sectors also received fairly high state subsidies) and also for inadequately prepared investment projects oriented primarily to CMEA markets (e.g., in the machine industry).

The efficient operation of the transformed banking system and of monetary policy was also impeded by the lack of change in ownership relations. The privatization of state assets began only in 1990, and even then, only at a slow pace. The cost and income sensitivity of enterprises remained low, and a great deal of administrative constraints were still enforced in the economy. True competition had not yet evolved, and the institutional system of the capital market was greatly underdeveloped. There was an excessive—often economically unfounded—demand for loans, and not even increasing interest rates could curb this for some time.

It should be noted that the NBH did not have sufficient experience in the application of market instruments of monetary policy, nor did the commercial banks in reacting to monetary policy or in establishing this new type of relationship with enterprises. Finally, the pressure exerted by national and local political forces also influenced the activities of the banks in 1987–1988. In that situation, the National Bank of Hungary employed a stringent, restrictive monetary policy. From 1987–1988, the money supply was reduced (as a percentage of the GDP), primarily by cutting refinancing loans, setting a relatively high reserve requirement, and gradually increasing the interest rates.

As a result of the particularly stringent monetary policy, the excess liquidity in the economy and the real value of domestic demand were reduced in 1988. From 1989, exports to CMEA countries also decreased. These developments—although favorable for the economy as a whole—had a deteriorating effect on the position of enterprises.

At the same time, other problems also surfaced. The large banks retained a relatively high ratio of substandard loans, which had been taken over mostly from the NBH in 1987. These loans include truly irrecoverable receivables that cannot be written off until the banks have accumulated sufficient risk reserves.

Commercial banks took some time to rationalize their lending practice. At first they continued to lend to loss-making enterprises with a very low credit rating, while profitable undertakings with good prospects frequently could not obtain the necessary credits. This was one of the reasons behind the irrational and widespread occurrence of inter-enterprise involuntary lending. Financial discipline deteriorated.

Enterprises in trouble because of their obsolete production structure, high cost production, and decreasing sales at first managed to siphon more and more credit out of the banks. Since 1989, when the banks began to follow more rational lending policies and took care to not let their substandard loans increase, disturbances started to emerge in the financial turnover of the economy. More rational lending policies, however, have positive economic effects, including improved financial discipline.

Inter-enterprise settlements were increasingly delayed, in part due to low interest rates prevailing in inter-enterprise lending. This led to the widespread deterioration of liquidity, affecting even otherwise healthy, profitable enterprises, which also could not recover their receivables. The phenomenon of "queuing" emerged: receivables "stood in a queue" at the debtor enterprises, and the enterprises at the banks. In 1989 the size of the "queue" grew particularly large, but it did not increase significantly in 1990.

Obsolete accounting and liquidation regulations and creditors' lack of attention to the problem made it possible for loss-making enterprises to continue to survive, thereby allowing this cancerous phenomenon to remain. Of course, this phenomenon also reduced the efficiency of monetary policy, as it resulted in the creation of "quasi-surplus money."

The relatively high and accelerating inflation had a negative influence on the lending activities of the banks, on the composition of their lending portfolios according to maturity, on the level of the interest rates, and, hence, on their relationship with their clients. (In 1990, the level of producers' prices increased by 24%, that of retail prices, by 29%.)

Nevertheless, the efficiency of monetary policy and the operation of the entire banking system improved considerably in 1990. The stringent monetary and fiscal policy eliminated the monetary surplus, contributed significantly to the improvement (of more than US $1.6 billion) of the external balance of payments surplus, and curbed the acceleration of inflation. The transformation and liquidation of loss-making enterprises has begun, albeit slowly. Loans and other services provided by banks greatly contributed to the large increase in the number of small-scale enterprises.

The increase in the number of commercial banks and banks operating with foreign participation and the intensification of competition made bank operations more flexible and facilitated the improvement of the quality of their services. Still, Hungarian banks are far from being able to meet the requirements of modern banking. The development of services is impeded by the inadequate branch network and the lack of modern technical instruments and technological knowledge.

The development of the banking system in recent years was also related to the appearance of the capital market. The number of joint-stock companies greatly increased in 1990, with more and more securities appearing on the market. The stock exchange was also established and has been functioning since. Nevertheless, the implementation of true money and capital markets is still in its initial stages.

Many measures are needed in all areas for the development of an advanced market economy in Hungary. One of these necessary measures is the completion of the transformation of the banking system.

D. The Implementation of the Market Economy

The view that the economy had to be fully transformed into a market economy gained general acceptance in early 1989 in Hungary. This recognition was followed by significant reform measures throughout 1989–1990. The political and economic changes that have taken place since provide favorable conditions for the completion of the process.

Following the free elections of March–April 1990, Hungary established a system of parliamentary democracy. The new government, the opposition parties, and all other social forces are fully committed to the establishment of a social market economy based on free enterprise as soon as possible. Based on the thorough preparatory work of the government, parliament is conducting a highly intensive legislative program to create the legal framework for a market economy. The Hungarian government is developing political and economic relations with other countries to gain their understanding and support during the transformation to a market economy. Additionally, the Hungarian government hopes these improved relations will help facilitate the process of market transformation.

The process of establishing the institutional framework of the market economy made major progress in the last few decades and especially in the second half of the 1980s. This process is expected to speed up and perpetuate itself over the next two or three years.

The program for further transformation of the Hungarian economy envisages the completion of an institutional system of a market economy (even if the process of privatization may take a few years longer to complete) and the stabilization of the economy by 1994. This program takes into account the consideration that the Hungarian economy has already covered more than half of the road leading to the market economy (more with respect to certain elements and less regarding others), but also that the economy, more or less stabilized by 1990, is going to be subject to severe shock effects in 1991 (especially as far as the country's relations with the former CMEA countries are concerned). However, the program's radical structures will counteract the negative consequences of the shock effects within two or three years.

The Hungarian economic program is not shock therapy. Shock therapy is neither necessary (as there is little domestic disequilibrium, no uncontrolled inflation, and the liberalization of imports, prices, and wages, and the reduction of state subsidies, etc., are about to be completed) nor politically possible (the problems to be solved, primarily privatization, cannot be handled in this manner). At the same time, the program does call for radical measures to be implemented in continuous stages (in particular, stringent monetary and fiscal policies). This policy is one of planned radical transformation, scheduled in a continuous (in certain justified cases, gradual) fashion, and not a policy of gradualism, as it is sometimes incorrectly referred to.

The greatest progress has been made in the development of *market relations*. The control of economic activity through mandatory state plans and the central allocation of resources by the state were abolished long ago. Enterprises are fully independent. The state has no part in concrete economic decision making. The foundation of new undertakings in a wide variety of forms, including both private ventures and foreign trading activities, is exempt from licensing requirements. The state facilitates and financially supports the foundation of new firms, the development of small enterprises, and especially the operation of private ventures.

With the initiation of the trade liberalization program in 1989, virtually all imports (more than 90% of expected industrial imports) and essentially all prices had been liberalized by 1991. Import liberalization as well as wage liberalization will be completed in 1992. (This relatively rapid liberalization process could be accomplished rationally only with a strict monetary policy.)

There is now a law forbidding unfair market behavior; the Cartel Office supervises adherence to this law with particular emphasis on the observance of antimonopoly measures. Privatization has also increased the number of competing firms.

The *privatization* of state enterprises is the key issue in the establishment of the market economy. For this reason and also because this process only began in 1990, the speedy and rational implementation of the privatization process will be the greatest and most difficult task of transformation in the years to come. The process is controlled by the State Property Agency, although privatization may also be initiated by the enterprises concerned as well as by the potential buyers. In fact, in the near future, privatization will be initiated and administered primarily by the enterprises concerned. Only the privatization of the largest, most important state enterprises will be directly organized by the State Property Agency. In other cases the agency will exercise only general, normative "control" over the process. Privatization is generally carried out by way of sale (that is, not free of charge); the acquisition of shares and business shares is facilitated by preferential loans and tax concessions. The intention is to reduce the share of state ownership in the competitive sphere of the economy to below 50% by 1993.

The influx of foreign capital and its participation in privatization is facilitated by a special law. Apart from a few exceptions, the foundation of companies with foreign capital having a share is exempt from any licensing obligation irrespective of the size of the share, although participation in the foundation of banks is still subject to licensing. Joint ventures enjoy tax concessions that are quite significant in certain activities if the profits are reinvested in Hungary. For joint ventures, imports and wages are already fully liberalized; the repatriation of capital and its earnings is also entirely free.

The *transformation of the financial system*, the third component in the establishment of the market economy, began in 1988. Following the tax reform of 1988, the structure of taxation now essentially corresponds to those of West European countries. In 1992–1993, tax rates and detailed rules are also expected to be established in a similar manner.

Subsidies from the budget are to be reduced to below 7% of the GDP in 1991, and to 4% in 1993. The reform of public finances (also including the transformation of the welfare system) is under preparation and will be implemented in 1992.

The continuation and completion of the reform of the banking system is linked to the full establishment of the market economy. This involves two objectives. First, full autonomy must be guaranteed to the National Bank of Hungary; government control over the bank must be abolished. Market methods should become the general instruments of monetary control: the role of distributive methods of refinancing should be cut further and then abolished, the share of open market operations should continue to increase, interest rates of the financial institutions should be fully liberalized, and the development of a uniform market-rate level should gradually be made possible; a domestic interbank foreign exchange market should be established and thereby the movement of exchange rates should be on a market basis. While using market mechanisms, the National Bank of Hungary will have to pursue a strict monetary policy as well.

Second, the increased role of foreign and private capital in commercial banks should be encouraged. This will also facilitate privatization in this area. The services of the banks will have to be improved considerably. Retail banking and foreign exchange operations are to be organically integrated into the activities of the commercial banks. To protect the interests of deposit holders and to ensure safe operation for the banks, international norms should be enforced in their management. Substandard loans are to be qualified according to these norms; sufficient provisions are to be set aside against them and irrecoverable debts must be written off. The State Banking Supervisory Board will have to act effectively and efficiently. (These issues are discussed in more detail in the following sections.)

In 1991 the parliament enacted two laws contributing to the

reform of the banking system: one on the National Bank of Hungary, the other on the financial institutions and their activities. Both laws will take effect January 1, 1992 and will take into account the experiences of the advanced countries. The latter will also consider the prescriptions of the Bank for International Settlements (BIS). Together with the laws on public finances, the capital market, (i.e., the laws regulating the stock exchange and the activities of investment companies), and the new laws on accounting and bankruptcy, these laws, in accordance with the activities of the market agents, will be extremely important in the development and operation of the market economy.

■ II. The National Bank of Hungary and Monetary Control

A. The National Bank of Hungary

The Parliament of the Republic of Hungary enacted the law on the National Bank of Hungary in October 1991. This will regulate the legal standing, tasks, relations, and organization of the NBH in an up-to-date manner. According to the bill, the National Bank of Hungary will be the central bank of the national economy and the central organ of the lending system and of foreign exchange management.

According to the new principle of the relationship between the NBH and the state organs, the National Bank of Hungary will be autonomous and will not be under the supervision of the government. Once a year it will report to parliament, though this does not mean that parliament can intervene in the NBH's business decisions. At the same time, the bank will support the implementation of the government's economic program (in the development of which it also takes part) with the monetary instruments it has available. There is, however, an important provision in the law: the NBH will at all times carry out its tasks and responsibilities as laid down in the law; it will not be instructed to act contrary to this. If the NBH deems that the economic policy or practical activities of the government endanger the stability of the economy, the NBH is obliged to warn the government and, if need be, to turn to parliament and to the public.

The basic task of the National Bank of Hungary is to protect the internal and external purchasing power of the national currency (the forint). It will have an exclusive license to issue bank notes and coins. The bank will resolutely represent this objective to the government in developing the objectives of a general economic policy and will enforce it in its monetary policy.

The National Bank of Hungary will independently formulate its monetary policy and the instruments thereof. These will aim at upholding monetary equilibrium, thereby facilitating the equilibrium position of the entire national economy. The NBH will influence the money and credit supply and demand through the control of financial instruments. The instruments of monetary policy will include refinancing (i.e., lending to commercial banks), regulation of the reserve requirement of the financial institutions, influencing or determining exchange rates and interest rates, and open market and other operations.

The National Bank of Hungary will keep the accounts of the state and its central organs and may keep the accounts of other budgetary organs. This latter activity will be gradually taken over by commercial banks.

It is extremely important that the law stipulate the principles of lending relations between the NBH and the budget, the practical implementation of which will be controlled by parliament. The law states that the total amount of loans granted by the NBH in a given year to the budget will not exceed 3% of the revenues of the central budget in the given year. (This provision will come into effect gradually, in a few years' time.) As of 1991, the interest charged on these new loans will correspond to the base rate of the National Bank of Hungary. (The preferential rates on the loans taken by the budget before 1991 will, however, remain valid.) The NBH will also act as the primary agent with respect to securities issued by the state, selling and buying such securities.

As the central organ of foreign exchange management, the National Bank of Hungary will regulate the lending and foreign exchange operations of the financial institutions related to external economic relations. It will also take part in developing the principles and conditions under which export credits are granted. Foreign credits (not including government credits) will either be taken out by or granted by the NBH, or the NBH will permit other financial institutions to perform these transactions. In practice, the latter will play an increasingly important part, and increasingly on the basis of general licenses. The National Bank of Hungary will develop the national system of payments and settlements, regulate financial turnover, and operate an information and control system.

In accordance with the principles of collaboration between the National Bank of Hungary, the government, and the parliament, the National Bank of Hungary will participate in the development of the government's economic policy and the government's annual budget bill, and it will present the principles of its own monetary policy to the government and parliament. The organs concerned will jointly ensure that the contents of the documents mentioned are harmonized. The president of the NBH will be invited to government meetings whenever the government discusses matters related to NBH activities. There will be a regular exchange of information between the government bodies and the National Bank of Hungary, which will cooperate with the State Banking Supervisory Board and the State Securities Supervisory Board.

The National Bank of Hungary will operate as a company limited by shares. All shares will be held by the state. Following the enactment of the law, the state as shareholder will be represented by the minister of finance.

Contrary to earlier practice, the president of the National Bank of Hungary will be appointed by the president of the republic, upon the recommendation of the prime minister, for a term of six years. The president of the National Bank of Hungary can be removed only on grounds set out in the law. He or she will be assisted by vice presidents. The organs of the NBH will include a meeting of shareholders, the board of directors, and the supervisory board. The council of the National Bank of Hungary will function as the supreme body controlling monetary policy, under the chairmanship of the president of the NBH. Members of the council will include the vice presidents of the NBH and a corresponding number of other individuals. They will all be appointed by the president of the republic, upon the proposal of the prime minister. On the basis of the new law, the legal standing of the National Bank of Hungary, its position, tasks, and the instruments it employs will essentially correspond to the practice of countries with advanced market economies.

B. The Instruments of Monetary Control

Monetary control in Hungary is directed primarily at regulating the money supply and the net domestic loan stock. After the banking reform of 1987, the NBH combined and applied instruments of monetary control so that the relationships of banks and enterprises would be based on economic principles that did not disturb the functioning of the economy. For this reason, the new banking system began to work with a relatively significant degree of "central redistribution": on the one hand, the NBH set a relatively high mandatory reserve ratio for the banks; on the other hand, the refinancing loans provided by the NBH attained major significance among the lending sources of the banks. Refinancing loans had to be given a major role, because enterprises (like households) had a relatively low propensity to save; the deposits they kept with commercial banks did not represent major proportions. In this period, the ratio of refinancing loans among the liabilities of commercial banks generally exceeded 50%, and in the case of certain large banks, 70%.

Later, enterprise deposits increased and the banks also began accumulating household savings. This made it possible (and the stringent monetary policy made it necessary) for the ratio of refinancing loans to be reduced. In 1990, this ratio decreased on average to 15%, and when calculated with the refinancing against foreign exchange deposits, to 19%. (NBH refinancing is much lower than the average in the case of short-term loans and higher in the case of loans with maturities exceeding one year.)

In the spirit of a restrictive monetary policy and in the interest of strict control of demand (necessitated by the process of liberalization), the National Bank of Hungary regulated the money supply so that its growth rate was less than the growth of GDP at current prices. The NBH not only reduced the relative magnitude of the refinancing loans, but also raised the base rate several times. In view of the fact that until the end of 1990 the NBH did not pay interest on mandatory reserves, a relatively large margin developed between the deposits of commercial banks and the loans provided by them. In this way, a relatively high lending rate evolved and was regarded by the enterprises as an inflation-generating factor. So long as there was a relatively high demand for credits, lending rates truly functioned this way in practice, and not as decisive inflation-curbing factors. From 1990 on, however, the results of the strict demand control over fiscal and monetary policies became visible, and the acceleration of inflation was slowed.

The development of the monetary processes in 1990 was

not, however, free of problems. Control of the money supply slackened in the last two months of the year. Enterprises obtained revenues from East European exports that were higher than expected (and still settled in ruble terms). Banks could then use the forint value of the increasing foreign exchange deposits for lending purposes. For this reason, the money supply ultimately increased faster than the GDP in 1990. As a result of restrictive monetary policy introduced at the beginning of 1991— namely, the reduction of refinancing loans, the contractionary money market operation, higher interest rates, and also changes taking place in foreign trade—the money supply index decreased substantially by the end of the first quarter of 1991 (in comparison to the same period of the previous year), reaching the 23%–24% foreseen in the annual program. The "surplus money" that had appeared for a short time disappeared.

In April and May 1991, the money supply and lending on the part of commercial banks began to pick up again, with the money supply exceeding that of the same period of the previous year by 26%–27%. The main reason behind this was that the amount of foreign exchange deposits collected by commercial banks from both enterprises and households increased. These had to be deposited with the NBH, but the NBH provided refinancing loans in the same forint amount. To tighten monetary regulations, the NBH extended the mandatory reserve requirement also to the foreign exchange deposits and raised the interest on refinancing loans made available against foreign exchange deposits. In addition, it reduced normative refinancing and tightened the rules for the generation of mandatory liquidity provisions. As a result of these measures, it is expected that the rate of increase in the money supply will fall below that of the nominal value of GDP and will be in line with the annual program.

The primary objective of monetary policy continues to be ensuring economic equilibrium and protecting the value of money. In 1991, the Hungarian economy can expect a major deterioration in its terms of trade with the Soviet Union and other Central and East European countries, and therefore a major reduction in its exports to those countries. Consequently, it is expected that the balance of payments—which was balanced in 1990—will temporarily show a deficit in 1991. In order to counterbalance roughly half of the losses to be suffered in 1991 and the remaining half in 1992–1993 through adjustment to the changed conditions, money will again have to be withdrawn from the economy. It will also be necessary to curb the inflationary process resulting from the rise in energy prices and the reduction of subsidies in 1991.

The National Bank of Hungary intends to make flexible, market-type control of the money supply predominant and to have quotas and the like replaced by market methods. Presently, the methods of monetary control to be employed in 1991 are elaborated in an unambiguous manner.

1. The Mandatory Reserve Requirement

The mandatory reserve requirement is an indirect instrument of control affecting the money supply. According to the prescriptions of the National Bank of Hungary, the banks have to set aside provisions on the deposits and settlement deposit accounts they keep and the securities they issue with a maturity, and to deposit these reserves with the NBH. The mandatory reserve ratio is presently 16%, to be satisfied daily. As of 1991, the banks will earn an interest on their mandatory reserves that now equals 50% of the base rate; the rate on foreign exchange deposits will be the market rate.

2. Refinancing

In 1991, the relative weight of regulation via the refinancing loans granted to the commercial banks will remain significant within the monetary policy of the National Bank of Hungary. At the same time, the National Bank of Hungary will continuously reduce the ratio of loans allocated on a quota-like basis, and to facilitate the rapid transformation of the economy, it will make the conditions for long-term loans more favorable than short-term ones. The NBH grants various types of short-term loans (with a maturity of less than a year) and long-term loans (with a maturity of over a year).

The purpose of *long-term* refinancing loans is to facilitate the restructuring effort and specifically the development of export-oriented production, privatization, and development of private enterprise. Accordingly, the NBH grants refinancing loans for the following concrete objectives:

- to supplement the loans given by international financial institutions (World Bank, International Finance Corporation, European Bank for Reconstruction and Development, etc.) aimed at the restructuring of the economy (naturally, in addition to re-lending these loans), up to 40% of the foreign sources;

- to finance investment projects aimed at setting up export capacities promising a fast return, on average up to 50% of the lending given by the banks;
- to provide coverage for medium- and long-term export trade credits, provided that their return is guaranteed;
- to facilitate, in relation to the sale of state assets, the acquisition of state assets and the development of the assets acquired (at preferential conditions);
- to supplement the loans provided by the banks for the development of small and medium-sized ventures.

The NBH provides *short-term* refinancing loans to supplement the sources available to the banks within the year. The role of individual and the so-called normative refinancing loans has already been reduced and will virtually cease in the near future (naturally, with the exception of the rediscounting of drafts), while lending by auction will increase in importance.

The normative refinancing loans are allocated by the NBH in proportion to the equity of the commercial banks, in part as a normative credit on current account (this was 10% of the equity of the banks in early 1991, reduced to 5% in mid-1991; it will be abolished in 1992) and in part as a credit line for draft rediscounting (this also takes into account the seasonality of the borrowing needs of the economy).

The National Bank of Hungary grants refinancing loans to the banks as short-term trade credits only for export deals supported by bank guarantees, in the period before delivery until the receipt of the compensation. A further specific form of refinancing by the National Bank of Hungary is that, as already mentioned, the banks place their foreign exchange deposits with the NBH and, in exchange, having met the mandatory reserve requirement, they can receive forint refinancing.

Since 1989, the banks have been able to obtain a part of their refinancing loans on a market basis at auctions held at regular intervals. The National Bank of Hungary decides on awarding refinancing loans on the basis of offers made by the banks on the amount and interest conditions of the loans. (Through the offers, the NBH can also get information on the liquidity position of the banks, their demand for credit, and their expectations as to interest rates.) In 1991, an increasing part of the short-term refinancing loans are being awarded through auctions.

3. Open Market Operations

To make monetary control more flexible, the National Bank of Hungary has, since 1989, been taking an active part in the market of securities operations. This method, however, can exert only a modest influence on the monetary processes.

Presently, the National Bank of Hungary, as proxy of the state, sells discounted treasury notes at auctions and to banks. In addition, the NBH places deposit notes on the market, whereby it can influence the liquidity of the financial institutions.

The fact that commercial banks do not yet have sufficient securities has a negative effect on the open market securities operations and, within these, on the activities of the National Bank of Hungary. It is expected that securities will be more widespread in the future, and then the NBH will be able to pursue monetary control in the secondary securities market to a greater extent.

4. Interest Rate Policy

Apart from a few exceptions, the National Bank of Hungary does not set mandatory interest rates or interest limits on loans provided or deposits collected by the banks. The NBH influences the level of interest rates by controlling the money supply and through the refinancing rates.

The National Bank of Hungary aims at a market-based, unified interest system. This, however, cannot be implemented at the moment, for three reasons. First, preferential interest rates are expedient and beneficial for assisting in the transformation of the economy, particularly in privatization and the enlivening of enterprises as well as exports. Second, the budget receives its credits at relatively preferential rates. Third, some of the housing loans taken out by households still bear preferential (i.e., subsidized) interest rates (to be abolished in 1992).

The base rate is decisive for the credits provided by the NBH. In this respect, the NBH enforces an interest policy in accordance with market forces by adjusting the base rate to the market rate on at least a quarterly basis. The level of the base rate is, naturally, lower than that of the prevailing market rates. The National Bank of Hungary charges the base rate on refinancing loans with a maturity of over a year and on the credits granted to the budget as of 1991.

The National Bank of Hungary applies preferential interest

rates (lower than the base rate) only for a narrowly defined circle, namely, loans linked to privatization and export credits (in the latter case, the interest is adjusted to international rates). In the case of short-term refinancing loans, interest rates enforced are at or near market rates.

Presently, the base rate is 22%; the preferential rate on loans linked to privatization is 75% thereof (that is, 16.5%). The interest rate on refinancing loans with a maturity of less than a year provided to financial institutions is currently 29%, and the rediscounting rate on drafts is 27%–29%. However, the interest rates that evolved at refinancing loan auctions is around 35%. The interest rate on refinancing loans provided against foreign exchange deposits is also close to 35%. (Also note that in 1991, producers' prices are expected to rise by 30%–32%, and retail prices, by 35%–37%.)

As of 1991, the NBH pays interest on mandatory reserves. Until the end of 1990, the NBH had set top limits on household deposit rates. In order to encourage household savings, this limit was abolished in 1991 for household deposits fixed for more than six months. The NBH encourages the conditions for the development of net positive real rates and thereby for better incentives for savings. We will return to the lending rates charged and deposit rates paid by commercial banks in section IIIA.

5. Exchange Rate Policy and the Foreign Exchange Market

The National Bank of Hungary determines the exchange rate of the forint against a basket of foreign currencies according to a system developed with the government. The NBH changes daily the quotation of the exchange rates of convertible currencies, in accordance with their movements on international money markets.

In the future, exchange rates will develop in the market. As a first step to this end, the proposal on the establishment of the interbank foreign exchange market is under preparation, the implementation of which will be a major step towards the full convertibility of the forint. According to this proposal, the obligation of the banks to sell foreign exchange to the NBH would at first be significantly reduced and later fully abolished. Commercial banks would trade foreign exchange on a market basis. The NBH would at most determine median exchange rates for the various currencies; the contract rates could then fluctuate within a determined range.

It should be noted that several steps will be taken in 1991 to liberalize foreign exchange operations (in addition to the import liberalization mentioned earlier):

- commercial banks will be able to take out foreign financial loans;
- entrepreneurs and commercial banks will be able to take out foreign loans for their development projects and current imports;
- foreign suppliers may be reimbursed for their imports also in forints, which they will be able to use freely inland (for, inter alia, the purchase of goods to be exported).

■ III. Commercial Banks and Specialized Financial Institutions

A. Number, Distribution, and Ownership Relations of Banks

As of July 1991, there are 37 commercial banks and specialized financial institutions operating in Hungary. (They had numbered 33 at the end of 1990; four new banks have been established since.) Of these, 31 have a general license and six are specialized financial institutions. Of the generally licensed banks, five can be qualified as large banks. (The generally licensed banks provide all banking services, the specialized financial institutions only a determined range of these services.) A few other banks are just being established; one new bank was founded in July 1991.

Banks can operate only in the form of companies limited by shares. The shares of the bank are held partly by the state, partly by enterprises, and partly by domestic and foreign financial institutions. The direct share of the state within the share capital of the banks has been gradually decreasing in the course of the past few years, to about 33% by the end of 1990. Thirty-five percent of the banks' capital is in the hands of enterprises and cooperatives, and 15% is held by other financial institutions. Foreigners hold 11% of the share capital of the banking sector. In the case of the large banks, it is characteristic that 33%–50% (on average 42%) of their shares are held by the state. The state has an approximately 50% holding in two of the small and medium-sized banks, while its share in the others is low or none at all.

There are, however, two specialized financial institutions in which the state holds at least 50% of the shares.

It is obvious that the share of the state's holdings in the equity of the banks is excessive and that it should be reduced not merely by raising the capital of the banks but also by selling the state's shares. The shares of the present state enterprises will be transferred to other forms of ownership, partly through privatization and partly through the sale of these holdings.

There are altogether 16 banks with a foreign share in the capital. In five of them, the foreign party has a holding of 20% to 45%, in another four, 50%, and in the remaining seven, 61% to 100%.

According to the bill on financial institutions and their activities, the approval of the State Banking Supervisory Board and of the National Bank of Hungary will be required for the foundation of any financial institution. To gain this approval, the financial institution will have to meet the economic, material, and staff requirements set forth in the law. No constraints are placed upon the participation of domestic private capital in financial institutions. However, Hungarian private capital and particularly natural persons have as yet hardly acquired any bank shares. In the future, the objective will be to create more favorable conditions to encourage the inclusion of private capital in the holding of the shares of financial institutions.

Economic policy also encourages the increasing participation of foreign capital in the foundation of new financial institutions and in the privatization of existing ones. Similar to the practice of other countries, special rules will be enforced: to establish financial institutions held in part or in full by foreign shareholders, the approval of the government in agreement with the president of the National Bank of Hungary will be required. The foundation of such financial institutions will be particularly desirable if they contribute to the improvement of services through the application of advanced banking methods and techniques and the setting up of branch networks throughout the country. For this, the foreign partner will have to have not only the necessary capital but also a good business reputation (goodwill) and satisfactory economic results. This may facilitate competition among the banks, which is a particularly important objective.

In order to demonopolize the banking system, the government, at present, encourages the participation of foreign capital in small and medium-sized banks and in the specialized financial institutions. The sale of the shares of large banks on a large scale to foreigners is not presently seen as desirable (until the banks become stronger and their balance sheets are cleaned up), but in 1992, the government will encourage banks to involve foreign participation in raising their prime capital. Thereafter a comprehensive program for large-scale privatization will be initiated.

B. Certain Economic Characteristics of the Banks

The structure of the banking system changed considerably and favorably in the years 1987–1990. The processes of demonopolization and deconcentration have made progress, evidenced by the increase in the number of banks and also by the decrease in the ratio of the large banks in the total assets of all the banks from 58% in 1987 to 52% in 1989 and to 48% in 1990 (Savings Bank not included). By an international comparison this ratio is still high. At present, the share of medium-sized banks is 15%, while that of the Savings Bank is 35%.

The total assets (liabilities) of the banking system amounted to 1,620 billion Hungarian forints (HUF) at the end of 1990, increasing by 26% relative to the previous year. The ratio of their own funds to the total was 7.5%; that is, the banks operate with a 92.5% external leverage, on the whole. (Medium-sized banks and the specialized financial institutions are better provided with equity than the average.)

The equity of financial institutions increased considerably over the past few years, reaching HUF 115 billion in 1989, about 5.5% of the GDP (but the process of capital growth slowed in 1990). Within this, the share of the large banks decreased.

There were significant balance sheet adjustments within the commercial banking system. Within the external liabilities of the banks, the enterprise deposits represent the most significant part, making up nearly one half of their total liabilities. (In the course of the last year, the deposits of small-scale entrepreneurs increased greatly.) The sale of securities increased at a dynamic rate. The share of securities within the leverage of the banks has reached 6%–7%, but it is still low. In line with the intentions of the National Bank of Hungary, the ratio of the refinancing loans within the liabilities of the banks has decreased, representing a mere 15% on average (this is 23% relative to the loan portfolios of the banks). The stock of foreign exchange deposits ("refinanced" by the National Bank of Hungary to the commercial banks in forint terms) increased substantially. The "refinancing" loans granted upon the foreign exchange deposits made up 3% of the total liabilities of the banks by the end of the year. The operation of the banks widened significantly in scope in 1990. This characterized both the structure of their services and their client turnover.

Within the context of the transformation of the economy, due to the reform of ownership and privatization, new business organizations were founded at an unparalleled rate. By the end of 1990, the number of business organizations doubled compared to the end of 1989, and tripled relative to the status two years before. This was concomitant not only with the large-scale increase in the banks' workload, but also with an increase in transactions related to banking costs and, furthermore, with greater risks for the banks owing to a large number of ventures just getting off the ground. At the end of 1990, the banks kept 110,000 accounts for 29,400 business organizations, which is 48% more than in the previous year (on average, each business organization has three or four bank accounts).

The distribution of client turnover is fairly differentiated mong the individual groups of banks: the three large banks keep 76% of the total number of bank accounts. The medium-sized banks, despite their large number, represent only a 6.5% share. Some of the foreign banks do very little by way of keeping accounts. The concentration of account keeping is due to several reasons. Several of the medium-sized banks do not as yet have suitable branch networks, hence their scope of movement with respect to client service and the keeping of accounts is limited. In addition, some banks are "selective" about their clients.

The range of services provided by financial institutions expanded significantly in 1990. This expansion is related to the decentralization of the foreign exchange operations and to the increase in the licenses linked to foreign exchange operations of the banks. Many commercial banks opened foreign exchange cash desks. Based on the special license of the National Bank of Hungary, five banks took out foreign loans independently and 12 banks are engaged in the administration of trade-related foreign exchange transactions. Several financial institutions have built up their foreign exchange lending operations.

The issue of short-term securities takes up a dynamically increasing share of the banks' activities, through which banks compete against one another in collecting funds from households. The banks' factoring operations have also expanded and credit card and automatic teller services were also introduced. No significant advance was made, however, in spreading retail banking operations, due to the fact that the majority of the recently established banks do not as yet have the necessary countrywide network.

Of the active lines of business, the most important one is lending: the banks' loan portfolios make up 65% of the total volume of the banks' active business. In the course of the past year, the loans granted to entrepreneurs increased by 31% on average; within this, short-term loans increased faster than the average, and those with a maturity longer than a year increased more slowly. The loans provided to small-scale entrepreneurs increased most dynamically, by 250%. Of the loans granted to entrepreneurs, 41% are long-term. Large banks provided 82% of the long-term loans, while medium-sized banks represented only 5%.

Presently, short-term lending represents an excessive share of the banks' loan portfolios. Demand for longer-term loans serving restructuring and modernization is low, mainly because of the lack of profitable and viable enterprise projects, the inadequate credit rating of certain enterprises, and the high interest rates arising from high inflation. Further, banks prefer to grant short-term loans, as the economic future of many large enterprises is uncertain, and the development of many of the new ventures is difficult to assess at this stage.

The banking sector joined in the financing of privatization. This is shown by the dynamic growth of lending to small-scale entrepreneurs; 77% of these loans are long-term. New undertakings are assisted by a number of special loan facilities.

Draft discounting and factoring, although increasing dynamically, still represent only a modest share in total lending. The increased market risks and the banks' attempt at lending with greater security are manifested by the fact that the amount of the bank guarantees assumed rose by 80%.

The *profits* of the banking sector grew at a rate somewhat faster than their turnover (by 28%) and reached HUF 63.3 billion. The profits to assets ratio of the banks approached 55% in 1990; the profits to total liabilities ratio was 3.9%. Within the profits, the net interest income, relative to the average lending of the banks, corresponds to an interest margin of 6%–7%. This may seem high in nominal terms, but it made up only about one-fifth of the interest rates and cannot be regarded as extraordinarily high under the inflationary conditions.

To protect the safety of the deposit holders and to mitigate their own risks as well as to be able to cover eventual lending losses, the banks did not disburse the larger part of their net profits as dividends, but set aside provisions instead. In 1990 (on the basis of the 1989 profits), 72% of the growth in their own funds was put to increase their capital reserves. A similar tendency was asserted also in the beginning of 1991, in the course of the allocation of 1990 profits.

The Hungarian commercial banks are still "undercapitalized." This is manifested by, inter alia, the facts that their branch network is underdeveloped, their technical equipment is not sufficiently modern, and their reserve capital has not reached the desired level. Therefore, in the coming years, the reasonable course of action will be not to reduce the interest margin and the profit but to capitalize reasonable profits as much as possible, besides increasing the reserves. On the other hand, this situation also makes the greater influx of foreign capital as well as of domestic private capital into the banking system desirable, primarily by way of the privatization and raising of the capital of existing banks, but also through the establishment of new foreign and joint banks or of Hungarian branches of foreign banks.

C. Interest Rates

The *lending rates* of commercial banks—in line with inflation and with the stringent monetary policy of the NBH—rose significantly. The characteristic level of these interest rates reached, on average, 24%–29%, depending on maturity, in contrast to the 17%–18% level in 1989. Interest rates, however, increased also in the course of the year, hence the year-end rates were higher than this. At the beginning of 1991, interest rates increased somewhat, but then this increase stopped. By mid-1991, the interest rate was 35%–36% for loans maturing within a year and 29%–30% for loans maturing over a year (with a very wide spread). In the case of discounted drafts, the characteristic interest rate was between 34% and 35%.

On average, the banks pay 29% on deposits fixed for less than a year to enterprises and 34% on deposits fixed for more than a year. Interest rates paid to households on deposits fixed for longer terms (and on securities) are around 30%–35% in general. Gross interests also include a 20% withholding tax, hence net (after tax) interests fluctuate between 24% and 28%; the net rate on sight or short-term deposits is between 17% and 21%.

Despite the fact that the real interest rate on household deposits was negative—which cannot be maintained in the long run—in the first half of 1991, the amount of household deposits increased at a dynamic rate. True, the greater part of this growth is shown by the increase in foreign exchange deposits, which is presently free of taxation, and interest rates are positive even in real terms. A positive or at least zero real rate on household deposits could evolve only if the withholding tax was abolished or at least reduced to a minimum, at least while the interest rate is not sufficient to ensure real increases in savings. The money market is unable to bear with significantly higher gross interest rates, as at higher lending rates it would not be possible to lend. It is expected that this problem will, with the curbing of inflation and the related reduction of interest rates, lessen in 1992.

D. The Problem of Substandard Loans

Both the substandard loans and the provisions of the banks increased significantly in the course of the past few years. Their ratio to one another is satisfactory in the case of small and medium-sized banks and specialized financial institutions founded in the past few years, all the more so as the share of substandard loans within their loan portfolios is not high and their balance sheets are in order.

The main problem lies with the banks that seceded from the National Bank of Hungary in 1987 and inherited a large volume of bad debts. At the end of 1989, even the declared amount of bad debts exceeded the amount of risk provisions in the case of the few banks belonging to this group. At the same time, it was established that their financial statements—prepared on the basis of the old Hungarian accounting regulations—do not give a true and fair view of the actual magnitude of the bad debts. For this reason, these banks were audited in 1990 by foreign auditors in order to qualify their assets according to internationally accepted criteria and also to evaluate the ratio of bad debts to risk provisions. The audits were repeated in early 1991 with respect to the 1990 balance sheets. The audits showed that although the problem does exist, its magnitude is much less than what was presented in the Hungarian and foreign press, and it is also less than similar problems in other Central and East European countries.

The Hungarian government, the National Bank of Hungary, and the boards of the banks concerned fully agree that all reasonable steps should be taken to put their balance sheets straight, for that is a necessary precondition for the healthy operation of the entire Hungarian banking system.

Therefore, in early 1991, the banks and later the government took measures that will result in the desired changes. First, based on new legislation, the banks revalued and qualified their assets strictly in accordance with international norms and accurately determined the magnitude of their bad debts and the related risks. Second, the banks determined the magnitude of the necessary risk reserves in line with international standards; these provisions were set aside in part in early 1991 to be completed in 1992 and 1993 (the banks paid relatively low dividends to their shareholders out of their fairly high 1990 profits—and this is what they will do also in 1991—in order to reach the necessary level of the risk reserve as soon as possible). Third, they will consistently write off their truly irrecoverable receivables as losses that will also be supported by the new accounting law. Fourth, the banks will cut back on their investments. Fifth, the state will also assist in the solution of the problems arising from the substandard loans originating before 1987 by putting the balance sheets of the banks straight by assuming partial guarantees. Sixth, the state will prompt these banks to raise their capital to reach the necessary capital adequacy.

There are three large banks that inherited relatively large volumes of substandard loans in 1987 and increased them further; therefore it has become necessary to clean up their balance sheets. These banks compiled their balance sheets for 1990, taking the opinions of auditors stated in mid-1990 into account, and decided on the distribution of their profits accordingly.

The total net assets of these three banks was HUF 43.3 billion at the end of 1990, of which the assets they could use as reserve amounted to HUF 9.2 billion; in addition, they also had provisions of HUF 1.4 billion. Their total liabilities amounted to HUF 551 billion, their profits to HUF 22.4 billion.

In total, these banks presented HUF 36.5 billion of substandard loans. At the same time, their reserve requirement—also considering the appropriate risk factors—made up HUF 28 billion. (These data were also confirmed by the new audits.) The actual reserves at the end of 1990 provided coverage for HUF 10.6 billion out of this. Approximately HUF 10 billion in additional coverage was generated by the fact that the banks paid relatively low dividends from their 1990 profits (10% in the case of two, and 8% in the case of one bank) but increased their capital reserves against this.

In order to reduce the need for provisions, if it comes to the actual use of the reserves, the budget, in accordance with the legal regulations in force, repays the profit tax paid by the banks in the course of the past few years before setting aside provisions (for it was not possible to set aside provisions before taxation for a temporary period). In addition, the state assumes guarantees at a determined amount (HUF 10.5 billion) for the substandard loans created before the banking reform and for 50% of the debts of the mining companies.

Based on the above, and if the necessary decisions are made, the substandard loans of the banks could be covered by the state guarantees and the reserves of the banks by the end of 1991.

There is, however, another uncertainty factor—because of the drastic cutback of exports to the Soviet Union, the economic position of certain enterprises that are unable to sufficiently increase their sales elsewhere may deteriorate to such an extent that bad debts of the banks may also increase. The magnitude of this problem cannot be foreseen at this time. Therefore it is expected that the law on financial institutions in 1992 will introduce a requirement to set aside provisions in accordance with international standards, but will allow the necessary level to be reached over a period of three years in all those cases where this cannot be ensured on January 1, 1992. In 1992, the capital adequacy requirement according to international norms (at first 7.25% and then 8%) will come into force. The banks will, in general, be able to comply with this requirement, although certain large banks will also need to raise their capital to accomplish this. In certain justifiable cases, the law will permit the Banking Supervisory Board to grant temporary exemption from compliance with the capital adequacy ratio on the basis of individual assessment.

The measures referred to will together ensure that the balance sheets of the Hungarian banking system (and within it, of the large banks concerned) will be straightened out and will comply with generally accepted international standards. This will certainly promote the relations of these banks with lending operations abroad, the introduction of their shares in the stock exchange, and the possibility that foreigners will play a more important part in the acquisition of their shares.

E. Further Regulations on Bank Activities and Banking Supervision

The law on financial institutions contains provisions that, fully in accordance with the regulations that will come into force in the European Community in 1992, safeguard the reliability of the system of financial institutions and the safety of the deposits they keep and of the financial processes. These include:

- rules pertaining to ownership that will limit the holding that a single owner may have as well as excessive cross-ownership;
- rules serving the safe operation of financial institutions, including provisions on the adequate magnitude of the equity, on capital adequacy, on liquidity, and on setting aside provisions;
- rules preventing the assumption of excessive risk by financial institutions that will, inter alia, restrict the ratio of large loans and various investments and make the insurance of deposits possible.

The law also contains provisions for the rules for competition among financial institutions as well as the rules to be applied if a financial institution is in danger, if it is becoming insolvent, and for its liquidation.

The State Banking Supervisory Board operates under the supervision of the government; its tasks and activities are determined also by the law referred to. The Banking Supervisory Board licenses the operation of financial institutions, supervises their compliance with the laws, and, if need be, introduces the measures so stipulated by that law.

F. Expected Development of the Commercial Banks

In the coming years, extraordinary and manifold changes are expected in the operation of the commercial banks as a result of the transformation of the entire economy. The demonopolization and the deconcentration of the banking system will continue. It is expected that additional commercial banks will be founded, primarily in the small and medium-sized category. These will probably include a significant number of banks with considerable foreign holdings. The large banks will also become stronger and develop, even if their relative role will be reduced. Interbank competition will become keener. The banks will significantly expand their branch networks and widen the range of services offered to both the business and the household sectors.

The change in the main lines of business of the banks will continue. The sectoral linkage that still exists in certain activities of the banks will disappear almost completely. The emergence of large numbers of new small and medium-sized ventures will cause major changes in the clientele of large banks. A significant number of banks are putting a great deal of effort and resources into participating in privatization-related lending, and several banks are preparing to provide general advisory services to entrepreneurs, making their operations more universal. This does not exclude the possibility of certain, especially smaller, banks concentrating their efforts specifically on a certain group of clients or banking services.

Given the fact that the privatization of the banks will proceed, and that the banks' shareholders will be diversified, particularly once their shares are introduced in the stock exchange, major changes will occur in the ownership relations of the banks. The reduction of the state's holdings in the banks will be served by the provision of the new law on financial institutions, which is expected to restrict the holding of a single owner to 25%. Thus the share of the state will, in the course of the coming years, be reduced primarily in the case of the large banks, partly through the issue of new shares and partly by selling a part of the shares of the state. The privatization of the decisive part of the state enterprises will "de-etatize" the shares held by them, too. In general, foreign and domestic private capital, also including natural persons, will play an increasing role in the ownership of the banks.

Another change needed in the operation of the banking system is that the ratio of *long-term lending* financing investments aimed at restructuring and modernization must be increased. This could be an important factor in giving new impulses to the economy. The increase in the role of long-term lending depends partly on the appearance of efficient and viable projects (to be expected upon the acceleration of privatization), but is also conditional upon the establishment of a few new specialized investment banks. (The foundation of such banks is in progress.) The ratio of refinancing loans provided by the National Bank of Hungary will continue to decrease. Hence the majority of the banks will want to obtain sources from households to a greater extent, will wish to increase enterprise deposits by extending their services, and will wish to raise further funds by issuing special short-term securities. A growing number of banks will obtain licenses to pursue foreign exchange operations; they will wish to widen their international contacts and increase their sources by collecting foreign exchange deposits and taking out foreign exchange loans.

The banks will have to introduce major changes in their operations as, within a few years' time, they will have to establish such ratios between their equity and deposits, and their receivables of various types and maturities, as to be able to satisfy the very strict requirements pertaining to the safety of operations and the protection of deposits. To this end, they will also set up a voluntary deposit insurance fund.

The increase in turnover of banks and the diversification of their activities will make it necessary for banks (including the smaller ones) to procure and adapt advanced electronic systems, apply modern procedures to perform and record their operations, and create an information base suitable for bank management. What is particularly important in this regard is that the banks speed up their transfer and other operations and that the non-cash methods of payment become widespread among households. The World Bank is also providing assistance to the Hungarian banks in these endeavors.

The joint national clearing center, to be established in 1992, will serve the interbank financial transactions. In addition to this, a national credit information system will be set up; this will greatly increase the safety of lending and make the infrastructure of the banking system complete.

On the basis of the above, the hope seems justified that the Hungarian banking system will, within a few years' time, be able to satisfy the requirements of an advanced market economy and of the money market with respect to both its structure and the mode of its operation.

■ *Postscript: The Curbing of Inflation and the Full Convertibility of the Forint*

It was mentioned that inflation in Hungary showed a tendency to increase over the period of 1989–1991. In 1989, the retail price level rose by 17%, in 1990 by 29%. In the first half of 1991, it exceeded the level of the first half of 1990 by 35%, and a similar rate of price level increase is expected for the entire year.

Inflation accelerated in 1991 primarily because imports (particularly of energy) from the former CMEA countries have become more expensive, price liberalization has been nearly completed, and state subsidies have been significantly reduced. In addition, the increase in wages, which attempted to offset the effects of inflation, had a major impact on the rise in prices (price-wage spiral) and so did the devaluation of the forint (price-exchange rate spiral) early in the year. That is, the acceleration of inflation is primarily due to a rise in costs, which can be curbed only to a limited extent by a stringent fiscal and monetary policy.

At the same time, the relative protection of the value of money, that is, the curbing of inflation, is a first priority objective of monetary policy and indeed, of the entire economic policy, not only because that is demanded by society, but also because high inflation deteriorates the efficacy of the various instruments of economic and monetary policy.

For this reason, the stringency of fiscal and monetary policies must be maintained: the budget deficit, and particularly its financing by the National Bank of Hungary, must be reduced, and the increase of the money supply must be less than the nominal value of the GDP. The share of household savings must increase among the lending sources of the banks (to debit refinancing by the NBH) and so must the share of loans granted to entrepreneurs within their lending portfolio (as against lending to the budget).

As far as wage increases are concerned, it would be expedient to aim at a social consensus that is not of a wage-indexing nature, but follows inflation only in part, resulting in moderate and decelerating wage increases.

In addition, an active but also cautious exchange rate policy should be pursued that reacts flexibly to the changes in the value of individual currencies (including the forint), but contributes as little as possible to the generation of inflationary expectations and inflation itself.

In view of the fact that actual export-import price levels are fully enforced within the Hungarian price system and the subsidy reduction program is near completion, once these conditions are fully met it is expected that not only the acceleration of inflation will come to a halt (this has in fact taken place in the first half of 1991), but it will also begin to decrease. In this case it is reasonable to expect that the increase of the retail price level will not exceed or will just exceed 20% and will decrease to below 10% by the end of 1993.

It is obvious that, in this case, a general and continuous reduction in interest rates will also follow. In addition to the beneficial effects on the entire economy, another result will be that economic agents will become more sensitive to monetary policy and its instruments. Therefore the propensity to save is likely to improve throughout the economy and so will the inclination to use money efficiently. This will not only increase the importance of the role of the banking system within the economy but will also render its operation more rational.

A highly important condition for turning the Hungarian economy into a market economy and ensuring the efficient operation of the banking system is that the forint become fully convertible. It is desirable to implement this within the shortest reasonable period.

What should be taken into account in this respect is that the extent of convertibility of the forint has already reached a relatively high degree. As far as current operations are concerned, the forint is almost fully convertible for Hungarian enterprises and entrepreneurs (as a result of import liberalization) and even more so for foreign investors (for whom all imports and the repatriation of the invested capital and the yield of that capital are fully liberalized). Foreign exchange purchases by households, capital operations of Hungarian residents, and trade in foreign exchange in the domestic market have not been freed as yet.

Obviously, it is more important to maintain full convertibility of the forint than to declare it. Inadequately grounded measures and declarations should be avoided so as not to have to modify them later. This requires thorough preparation followed by resolute and comprehensive measures, while caution and prudence should be exercised as far as declarations are concerned.

Full convertibility of the forint is conditional upon a number of important factors:

- the rate of inflation must be driven back to single-digit levels so as to avoid the frequent or constant devaluation of the forint;
- the country's economic performance must improve to the extent that the current account is essentially balanced in the long run and consequently (and also as a result of increases in exports and in capital imports), the debt to exports ratio must improve considerably;
- the country's foreign exchange reserves must reach the value of at least three to four months' imports so that unexpected events or emergencies will not endanger convertibility of the forint;
- the domestic interbank foreign exchange market must be established (not only must its system of operation be developed, but its technical conditions must also be implemented), and exchange rates must be formed by the market;
- appropriate conditions must be created in the economy and in the institutional system of the capital market for profitable domestic investments.

It can be seen from the above that full convertibility of the forint does not simply depend on decisions and is not a matter of declarations; it will be the result of an intensive process of many years. It should be noted that for a period of time, the exchange rate of the convertible currencies in the black market exceeded the official rate by a mere 5%–10%; that fact also supports the possibility of the relatively rapid completion of the convertibility of the forint. The forint will first become fully convertible for current operations and later also for capital operations.

The completion of the transformation of the Hungarian banking system and the improvement of its operations are important elements of this process. At the same time, full convertibility of the forint will greatly contribute to the organic integration of the Hungarian economy into the activities of the international banking system of the market economies of Europe and the world.

Main Data of the Financial Institutions (Commercial Banks)

	1987	1988	1989	1990
Change in GDP, in real terms, in %	103.9	99.9	99.8	94.0
Change in GDP in nominal terms, HUF bn	1,226.4	1,409.5	1,706.0	2,047.7
in %	112.6	114.8	121.0	120.0
Money supply (M2), HUF bn	599.0	620.0	700.0	900.0
change in %	110.2	103.5	112.8	123.6
NBH refinancing loans*				
—short-term	244.0	211.4	238.2	224.5
—over a year	160.9	152.1	152.7	159.2
Characteristic annual average market lending rates, in %		17–18	18–20	24–29
No. of financial institutions	21	23	27	33
Of this:				
—general license	5	5	13	26
—specialized financial institutions	16	18	14	7
of this: with foreign shareholders	3	3	8	13
Main indices of financial institutions, HUF bn				
—total assets	999.5	1,019.4	1,247.3	1,620.5
—equity	53.2	75.0	93.9	115.7
—profit	27.4	34.7	49.7	63.3

*without the National Savings Bank

Source: National Bank of Hungary

3

Problems in Czechoslovak Banking Reform
VLADIMÍR JINDRA

I

Banks in Czechoslovakia recognized long ago that the economic system prevailing under communist rule was doomed and that a transition towards the market was inevitable. We made several attempts to reform the most flagrant distortions in the system, only to find that every attempt to transplant some market elements into the centrally planned mechanism generated a nonviable hybrid. No matter how carefully we disguised our reform projects, our efforts were branded as counterrevolutionary every time and were brutally swept away.

Ever since the November 1989 "Velvet Revolution," however, Czechoslovak banking has acted as a locomotive drawing the other sectors towards the market. Perhaps this is because banks, money, credit, interest, exchange rates, etc., were so uncompromisingly degraded and humbled during the last four decades in Czechoslovakia. Money was nothing but a mirror that passively reflected for bookkeeping purposes the physical flows predetermined by the plan; banks themselves were deprived of an active role, and were condemned to act as obedient servants of "His Majesty the Plan." What we bankers are experiencing today is the rebirth of money and banking, a virtual renaissance of monetary functions. No more do we seek convergence between planning and the market as in the past; what we strive for is a genuine market economy without any additional

Vladimír Jindra is Adviser to the Governor of the State Bank of Czechoslovakia.

attributes. Given this background, it is understandable that the very first step taken after the revolution was the division of the formerly monolithic State Bank into a genuine central bank and a number of independent commercial banks—in other words, into a two-tier system.

Until recently, we watched with envy the Hungarian and Polish bankers, who were allowed to initiate reforms much earlier than we, and who could consequently spread their reform steps over a longer period of time and acquire experience through theoretical discussions and practical experiments. Unlike them, we have been forced by circumstances to concentrate our reform steps into an extremely short time span and, what is worse, to undertake those steps in the absence of our own theoretical research and our own experiments. We seek to offset this handicap by carefully studying the experience of our neighbors in order to avoid their mistakes.

Drawing directly on the experience of advanced Western economies and their banks is not as simple as it might seem, at least during the early transitional phase. Many books have been written on how to proceed from a market economy to a centrally controlled economy, but not a single one exists on how to do it the other way around. The sequencing of the reform steps is also important and must be tailored to every country's economic situation. These observations naturally pertain to economic reform in general and to the reform of the banking sector in particular. The advice and expertise under the technical assistance program of the International Monetary Fund is priceless to us. Czechoslovakia rejoined the IMF and the World Bank on September 20, 1990. Our entry should be regarded as a signal to the world banking community that we are serious about our economic reform and that the IMF vouches for our credibility by its generous and promptly delivered standby assistance for our reform.

II

Our reform steps must have an adequate macroeconomic framework. Our government has decided that the principal task of our macroeconomic policy is to establish an economic environment in which the unavoidable disturbances in the micro-sphere, caused by price structure changes and capital reallocation, are not translated into a further deterioration of global disequilibrium, into galloping inflation and excessive growth of foreign debt. The transformation processes must therefore be regulated in such a way as to prevent increased demand by households, enterprises, and the government from boosting the price level. The top priority of this policy is to block inflation; all the other economic targets, such as economic growth, maintenance of the employment level, and balance of payments equilibrium, are subordinated—in a reasonable way—to this priority. This policy follows from the assumption that in the presence of economic upheavals it would be difficult, if not impossible, to accomplish the reform. This approach has predetermined our fiscal and monetary policies, which are conceived as rigorously restrictive.

Our first postrevolutionary state budget ended with a moderate surplus. The state budget for 1991 will likewise generate a surplus (Kčs 8 billion, which is equivalent to about 1% of our GDP), mainly by reducing agricultural subsidies and defense and other expenditures. This goal is particularly demanding due to the pressure resulting from a contraction of output (due to armament production conversion and economic restructuring), from a decline in enterprise profitability, and from the rise in unemployment, which requires larger outlays for the social safety net. Yet it has turned out that, as a result of a one-time price revaluation of their inventories after the price liberalization, enterprises have achieved impressive profits even though their output was going down, and the larger profit tax yield brought about a much larger surplus in the state budget than envisaged. This unexpected surplus will be used to cut down the turnover tax rate in order to reduce consumer prices and boost the demand for consumer goods.

Hand in hand with an anti-inflationary state budget policy goes a restrictive monetary policy. We planned a very tight monetary corset for our economy for the year 1990: while national income was expected to rise by 2%, credits to enterprises were supposed to rise from -2% to +1%. For the first half-year we succeeded in accomplishing this goal. Due to unforeseeable outside factors (breakup of the CMEA, collapse of the USSR, unification of Germany, oil-price boost) and domestic factors (economic decline by 3%, two rounds of price adjustments, three devaluations), we ended with a credit expansion of 3%, which, under the circumstances, is regarded even by foreign bankers as a success. In order to achieve an efficient resource allocation, Czechoslovakia liberalized prices on January 1, 1991 for most items, both at the producer and retail levels. Today 90% of prices are free, and the regulation of the rest is expected to vanish soon. This price liberalization took place under conditions characterized by a serious deterioration in our terms of trade, higher oil and raw material prices, exchange rate adjustments, and repercussions from the Gulf war. All this led to a temporary price increase, which should be limited to the first three months of 1991 and then recede. In order to prevent this one-time price jump from turning into an inflationary spiral, the central bank adopted a particularly restrictive policy for this period, which has proven successful so far: from December 1990 to January 1991, prices rose by 25.8%, from January to February by 7.0%, from February to March by 4.7%, and from March to April by 2%. It appears that the price jump has already hit the ceiling of effective demand.

For the rest of the year, it is expected that prices will stabilize at a new lower level, while credit to enterprises and households will be extended somewhat more generously (by 23% for the year as a whole). It is expected that this policy will, on the one hand, prevent the triggering of an inflationary spiral and, on the other hand, keep bankruptcies and unemployment at a tolerable level. In other words: Friedman with a slight touch of Keynes.

The tight credit policy will be accompanied by higher interest rates, which should encourage savings and discourage borrowing. During 1990 the State Bank raised the discount rate four times, from 4% to 10% by the end of the year. In the future, the discount rate will be coordinated with interest rates on foreign currency deposits, which, in their turn, should be kept competitive with rates on international markets. With an eye to the discount rate, the commercial banks established a prime rate of 18% for loans to the best customers. A binding upper limit on credit rates was set by the central bank at 24% (discount rate plus 14%), which, in the meantime, could be lowered to 22% (discount rate plus 12%) as a signal to borrowers that the period of expensive money is over and that they can again consider expanding their production. In due course—as commercial banks start competing with each other—this administratively fixed maximum rate will be abolished and interest rates will be determined solely by the market. The interest rate on deposits should motivate savings, and therefore—with the exception of the first three months of 1991—the nominal rates will be kept above the rate of inflation. It is expected that in the long run, the commercial banks will keep the deposit rates at or slightly above the discount rate.

It goes without saying that the high interest rate policy has both supporters and opponents. High interest rates on credit are especially detrimental to the fledgling private sector and private entrepreneurs, who criticize even the preferential rates offered to them by commercial banks in the range of 16%–19%. The depositors are likewise dissatisfied. They desire interest rates on deposits above inflation in real terms. In our opinion, everything depends on the future course of inflation. Should there be an upswing—however violent yet confined to only a couple of months—we could probably dare to raise the rate only moderately. However, should inflation extend over the whole year (without a stabilization of prices after three to four months), then the raising of interest rates on deposits would be inevitable.

III

The State Bank of Czechoslovakia is systematically building up the traditional monetary policy transmission mechanisms typical for central bank-commercial bank relations: reserve requirements, rediscount and refinance policies, and dealings in specified securities. Banks existing prior to January 1, 1990 are obliged to maintain a capital/assets ratio of at least 1.5% and to improve this ratio to at least 2% by the end of 1991 (for savings banks this ratio is 1%). Banks founded after January 1, 1990 must reach a ratio of 8% (recommended by the Bank for International Settlements) before the end of 1991. In order to enable banks to cope with this target, the profit tax has been reduced from 75% to 55%, allowing the banks to build up their various reserve funds at a faster rate. Another instrument is the minimum compulsory reserves, which should amount to 8% of primary deposits and which the commercial bank must keep with the central bank, where they earn a 4% interest. This 8% ratio represents a monthly average. If it is lower, the commercial bank must pay a penalty to the central bank equivalent to a 20% interest (double the discount rate). Another instrument is the liquidity ratio, according to which long-term loans cannot go beyond 125% of the bank's short-term resources.

As we have little trust in these newly introduced indirect instruments, we continue to use credit ceilings as our chief weapon. These credit ceilings are only indicative (for orientation purposes) and they are regarded as a provisional instrument. When determining their scope, the central bank takes into account the lending capacity of the particular bank and the bank's own suggestions as to the size of the ceiling.

In 1990 the amount of new credits pumped into the economy was only 1%, although there was 10% inflation. For 1991 the credit ceiling was raised to 20%, although inflation is expected to run at 30%. This represents a 10% restriction. Even though this is extremely rigorous, the corresponding increase of credit amounts to Kčs 120 billion.

In order to keep the period of price adjustments after the price liberalization as short as possible, the central bank introduced a particularly rigorous credit squeeze for the first 3 months of 1991, allowing only a 9% credit increase (equivalent to Kčs 48 billion) as compared with the envisaged 30% price jump. Although this policy had immediately been exposed to criticism from all quarters (the central bank being blamed for having caused a recession), it turned out that the commercial banks failed to use even this narrow margin for making their lending more liberal and raised the amount of new loans by only 1%. It took the central bank a lot of time to persuade the commercial banks to ease their practices somewhat. The commercial banks were hesitant to do so, arguing that they see no creditworthy objects and that most of their clients are nonviable.

Another important tool of regulation is refinancing. Every commercial bank is entitled to obtain refinance credit from the central bank. It may use this credit as it wishes, up to a volume specified each month by the percentage of the bank's total lending to the amount of loans extended to all commercial banks, paying only the discount rate for this loan. Apart from that, the central bank organizes auctions once a month where a certain amount of refinance credit is made available to the representatives of commercial banks and extended to those who offer the highest interest. The central bank will change the current system of fixing the refinance volume according to the size of obligatory reserves and will introduce a more flexible approach to expanding the refinancing mechanism. In order to promote the use of bills of exchange for financing domestic trade (which are still an unknown instrument in Czechoslovakia), the central bank will charge a lower interest rate for discounting eligible bills than for discounting commercial banks' own promissory notes serving as collateral.

As regards the bank's foreign exchange sphere, the following binding targets have been set: the ratio of total foreign exchange assets to liabilities, the ratio of total foreign exchange liabilities to the bank's capital, and the minimum percentage of short-term foreign assets to short-term foreign liabilities. Yet this mechanism is in its fledgling stages and lacks credibility so far.

A *conditio sine qua non* for the indirect transmission system is the establishment of a newly conceived clearing and settlement system. The prevailing interbank clearing and settlement system is based on an automatic accommodation of interbank payment flows. It will be replaced in 1991 by a new system based on settlement accounts for every bank with the central bank. This will allow the central bank to steadily control the demand for and the supply of bank reserves and regulate this through indirect instruments.

IV

We know that we need a rational price system to serve as a yardstick for measuring efficiency and for the reliable allocation of resources. A rational price system can be brought about through price liberalization. In a small country such as Czechoslovakia (with many large monopolies), this is more easily achieved by the introduction of foreign competition than by breaking up the existing monopolies through bureaucratic procedures. We therefore must liberalize imports. In order to liberalize imports, we have to make our domestic currency convertible. It is clear that convertibility cannot be achieved and maintained without an initial devaluation. While everybody supported convertibility, there were, and still are, vigorous debates about the degree and intensity of the initial devaluation. Some economists advocated a small-scale devaluation, as this would not boost the domestic price level. Others argued that if the devaluation is only moderate, we will not be able to maintain the exchange rate without resorting to heavy borrowing abroad or devaluing the currency later on, which would deprive us of credibility in the eyes of the public. This school of thought favored a massive initial devaluation that would bring the exchange rate closer to the market rate. The exchange rate would promote exports, but, at the same time, through higher-priced imported inputs, would ultimately raise the domestic price level and lead to bankruptcies and unemployment.

As soon as our enterprises learned about the intention to

devalue the korunas (in September 1990), they immediately started to act as true entrepreneurs, using their accumulated foreign exchange holdings or their foreign currency claims to boost their imports, which shot up by 17% in the third quarter while exports remained unchanged. Moreover, the enterprises started paying promptly for their imports, refrained from using standard credits, and on the other hand—in anticipation of better exchange rates—they postponed the collection of their receivables until the time after devaluation when they would obtain more korunas for their exports. This behavior negatively affected the balance of payments and we had no option but to devalue the koruna in advance of the introduction of convertibility and of a system-oriented package of reform measures scheduled for January 1, 1991. Thus, a massive devaluation took place in mid-October 1990, and, on the verge of convertibility, only a moderate devaluation was effected. We introduced current account convertibility (described as internal convertibility) as a preliminary step to full convertibility.

Under the present internal convertibility, all restrictions on payments for imports have been removed, and such payments are being conducted by commercial banks if properly documented. Exporters are obliged to sell their foreign currency earnings to the commercial bank in exchange for korunas. So far the koruna is not tradable on foreign exchange markets, convertibility does not include capital account transactions, and citizens are excluded. The tourism allowance for citizens has been raised from Kčs 2,000 to Kčs 5,000 for the whole year (which represents about 160% of average monthly earnings). Citizens continue to maintain their foreign exchange accounts with Czechoslovak commercial banks. The two separate rates, the commercial rate and the tourist rate, were unified (meaning that the koruna was devalued for enterprises, and somewhat revalued for citizens). The present exchange rate is Kčs 28 to one US dollar. A 20% import surcharge was introduced as a transitional measure, representing an additional asymmetric devaluation for the importer of consumer goods and food. This import surcharge was later reduced to 18% and, more recently, to 15%, which should signal that the foreign exchange situation of the CSFR is satisfactory and that we can afford to encourage imports.

The black market foreign exchange rate, which in the past greatly exceeded the official rate, nowadays deviates from the official rate by only 2%–3%, which is another proof of a prudent foreign exchange policy on the part of the central bank. The explanation of why there is a currency black market at all lies in the fact that the amount of hard currency officially sold to Czechoslovak tourists is inadequate and must be supplemented from illegal, slightly more expensive sources.

The koruna has been pegged to a basket of currencies that play the primary role in Czechoslovak exports and imports and that will provide an anchor to domestic prices after their liberalization. In the future we would like to peg the koruna to the ECU. We have started listing the ECU rate for our enterprises, and we intend to conduct part of our trade with the former CMEA countries in ECU.

In order to protect the initial exchange rate during the first months after foreign trade liberalization, it was necessary to build up our foreign exchange reserves (which had been reduced to only US $1 billion on the eve of the introduction of convertibility) to an amount that would serve as a cushion and enable the central bank to intervene. The IMF is supporting our reform program by a massive standby arrangement in an amount equivalent to 105% of our quota; with a contingency element for oil in the amount of 25% of our quota; and a compensatory and contingency financing facility amounting to 82% of our quota, the latter to be activated in the event that oil prices become higher than envisioned. We also obtained a structural adjustment loan from the World Bank and loans from the EC and other members of the Group of 24. The development of the balance of payments is surprisingly good (thanks to lower imports, a result of the new exchange rate and the import surcharge). As a result, Czechoslovakia did not have to use the full amount of foreign loans and still kept its international reserves equivalent to two months' imports. Czechoslovakia is proud of its record as a debtor: it never defaulted, and it never applied for debt restructuring. This is why we have turned with confidence to world capital markets, where we intend to place our bonds, the yield of which would speed up the reform process and protect the success of internal convertibility (about US $300 million worth of bonds have been placed through Nomura Securities on the Japanese market). It is expected that additional funds will flow into the country in the form of direct investment, which, unfortunately, is lagging behind our expectations. External debt in convertible currencies (US $7.9 billion by the end of 1990) is expected to rise to US $11 billion by the end of 1991 (31% of GDP), and debt servicing will reach 11% of current account receipts in 1991. In April 1991 the IMF mission, after careful examination, came to the conclusion that all criteria, the fulfillment of which is decisive for further access to IMF standby facilities, had been fulfilled.

V

New banking legislation is to be approved by mid-1991: this will consist of a new statute on the State Bank of Czechoslovakia and a new statute on banks. The legislation on the German Bundesbank served as a model for the statute on the central bank, largely because of the high degree of autonomy that the Bundesbank enjoys and its outstanding record in safeguarding the stability of German currency. The Bundesbank's federative structure and the distribution of powers between the directorate and Landeszentralen can also be copied with respect to a recently adopted law concerning the competencies of the Federation and the Czech Republic and Slovak Republic, which can now be translated into monetary policy and the role and organization of the State Bank of Czechoslovakia.

The draft statute on the central bank proposes an autonomous central bank. However, in order to demonstrate that the central bank firmly stands behind the government's reform scenario and supports the implementation of the economic reform, the draft does not explicitly stipulate the central bank's independence from the government. Although independent of instructions from the government regarding monetary policy, the bank will support the government's general economic policy unless this creates insoluble conflicts with the objectives of monetary policy. While the State Bank will be responsible for the formulation and implementation of credit policy, with respect to foreign exchange policy it is responsible only for its implementation. The formulation of this policy is up to the government. The draft statute proceeds from the division of responsibilities among the federal government and the governments of the republics. In accordance with this, it conceives a single, uniform central bank, with a center for the Czech Republic and a center for the Slovak Republic. The draft statute further proposes a board of directors as the highest decision-making body. The composition of this board guarantees that both federal and republican interests are represented and productively participate in the policy formulation of the central bank. The board is headed by a governor, who rotates in office; in other words, if the governor is of Czech nationality, he or she will automatically be replaced by a Slovak citizen once his or her electoral cycle is over, and vice versa. The governor will be nominated by the president of the Czech and Slovak Federal Republic or by the federal assembly upon the recommendation of the government of the CSFR.

Normal business of the bank will be managed by a directorate composed of the chief officers of the bank. The directorate is responsible for the implementation of policies adopted by the banking board. Contrary to the views of the Federal Finance Ministry, the State Bank insists on being the sole supervisory and regulatory agency for banks operating on Czechoslovak territory. We argue that as long as the central bank functions as the lender of last resort to the banks, it must be empowered to supervise them and to revoke banking licenses whenever banking principles are violated.

The central bank will have the authority to issue its own securities and to purchase, sell, and deal in securities for its own account. The draft statute emphasizes the accountability of the central bank, obliging it to inform the public of its policies and to present semiannual reports to the parliament on monetary policy objectives and development. Unfortunately, during the work on the draft, much more time was devoted to the problem of federal and republican competencies, to the question of the unity of the central bank or the establishment of three central banks (one for the federation, one for the Czech Republic and one for the Slovak Republic), than to the reinforcement of the central bank's monetary functions.

The new draft statute places all banks, regardless of their legal form or type, on the same footing. Nor does it discriminate against foreign banks, which enjoy the same rights as the Czechoslovak banks. The draft foresees the future bank as a universal bank similar to German banks; in other words, unlike the US bank, the Czechoslovak bank is free to collect deposits and simultaneously invest in securities. License to the bank is issued by the central bank in agreement with the pertinent finance ministry. The central bank is expected to exercise supervision over the banks along the same lines as central banks in Western countries and lay down the prudential rules for commercial banks similar to those used by central banks of longer standing.

VI

Today there are 30 commercial banks operating in Czechoslovakia, which might seem adequate given our country's small territory. However, most of the newly established banks have no branch network, the client in the district being fettered to one single bank as before. The market is dominated by two large banks, which were severed from the former monolithic state bank a year ago and which inherited its district branches. Commercial Bank Prague accounts for 54% of the total volume of credit, and the General Credit Bank Bratislava for 22%; all the other banks share only a fraction of the financial market.

At present, we seek to improve the banking infrastructure, which suffers from many defects, the legacy of the past regime. The banks are undercapitalized: their capital/assets ratio is around 1% in our largest banks. The banks are oriented to specific groups of clients, to specific activities, or to a narrow territory. The scope of financial services provided by banks is limited: payments and settlements through banks are unreliable. The banks are understaffed, particularly if compared with banks in advanced countries; banks need computerization, buildings, and management and employee training. The introduction of new instruments presupposes a new accounting system in the banks and a new reporting system. On strict commercial terms, the creditworthiness of most enterprises is questionable. Rather than writing off their claims, the commercial banks will probably convert part of their claims into participation in their debtor's business. Some traditional banking tools are still unknown: for example, mortgage securities, bills of exchange, and bank drafts. Also, commercial banks are unable to apply prudent banking practices.

The following banking activities or products are either nonexistent or at an early stage of development: financial consultancy, strategic planning, portfolio management, and modern information technology. Leasing, forfeiting, factoring, franchise banking, and mortgage banking are absent or underdeveloped. Investment trusts, the role of which increases in importance with the forthcoming privatization, are spontaneously emerging without a proper legislative foundation.

Commercial banks (particularly the savings banks) seek to rid themselves of unprofitable loans that used to be, and still are, a part of the government's social policy package (to young couples and to persons financing the construction of their own dwelling). The banks are obliged by law to charge an extremely low interest on those loans; this interest covers only a fraction of the price they themselves have to pay for the deposits or refinance loans from the central bank. The resulting loss is refunded from the state budget, but still the loan is unprofitable. It goes without saying that sooner or later these loans must be replaced by something more transparent and less cumbersome.

A specific Czechoslovak problem is the existence of the so-called perpetual loans, which account for almost 20% of all loans. These are, in fact, a disguised form of indirect loans to the state budget. Some 25 years ago the state budget withdrew a major portion of resources from the enterprises and, although it refunded part of them later on, it still keeps most of them in order to avoid a deficit, which had been politically outlawed. As a result, the State Bank of Czechoslovakia, as the only bank at that time, was compelled to replace the missing amount by extending credit without maturity and at a low interest rate. Now, as market principles start to permeate our economy, the commercial banks ordered a repayment of those credits within a few months and started to charge normal market rate on those credits. As a result, most of the state-owned enterprises were threatened with bankruptcy and "raised hell." The way out of this dilemma was found by setting up a special Consolidation Bank founded by the Federal Finance Ministry, which took over a large part of these perpetual quasi-loans from the commercial banks (along with the resources serving as their collateral) and spread their repayment over a period of eight years, maintaining a low (subsidized) interest rate. The ultimate decision on this category of loans and the further existence of the Consolidation Bank will be made in connection with decisions on large-scale privatization. In the meantime, the balance sheets of commercial banks are cleaned of this substandard category of loans, their assets are lower, and their capital/assets ratio are, as a result, better.

An important role on the periphery of the Czechoslovak banking sector is played by the offices or agencies of several international financial institutions situated in the CSFR. First of all is the office of the International Finance Corporation, which uses Czechoslovak commercial banks as intermediaries to channel IFC loans to small and medium-sized private companies. These loans have a longer maturity than normal Czechoslovak loans and are linked to a three-year grace period. Since the private sector is still in its infancy, the IFC office at Prague considers it necessary at the present to assist in the process of privatization and in finding suitable foreign partners for selected Czechoslovak enterprises.

The European Bank for Reconstruction and Development, with headquarters in London, has also started doing business in the CSFR, primarily as consultant, coordinator, and co-investor.

A positive role in the Czechoslovak banking sector will be played by the Technical and Financial Advisory Unit, sponsored by the World Bank and founded as a joint-stock company owned in equal shares by Czechoslovakia's central bank and various ministries. It will make technical and financial recommendations to the commercial banks, evaluate the creditworthiness of their clients, and provide subloans to commercial banks, enabling them to extend loans with a somewhat longer maturity than is normally the case.

The dynamic development of the banking sector is hampered by the obsolete clearing and settlement system. In the sphere of non-cash payments among companies and organizations, the situation looks somewhat better than in the sphere of payments by citizens. The payments system is carried out by the largest commercial banks, which have relatively good technical facilities at their disposal. The payment system suffers from a large volume of inter-enterprise debt (arrears) which exceed Kčs 65 billion in spite of regular mutual compensations. This negative phenomenon is a legacy of the former centralized planning system, which neglected the role of money. As a result, companies kept ordering raw material, component parts, etc., even if they knew that they were unable to pay the bill. On the other hand, the supplier was interested in the fulfillment of the planned target and did not worry about collecting the money. As a result of this attitude, companies accumulated huge amounts of stock last year in anticipation of higher prices after the price liberalization and devaluation of the currency. The present sales difficulties (owing to the contraction of the CMEA market and lower demand on the domestic market after the price liberalization) only multiply their troubles.

Particularly lagging behind the world standards are payments by citizens. There are not more than 35,000 credit cards now in use in the whole country. Their number should double within the coming years. The establishment of an Interbank

Association for Credit Cards sponsored by six commercial banks is the first step in this direction.

There are only 68 automated teller machines in the branch offices of the Czech Savings Bank and 17 in the branches of the Slovak Savings Bank.

Czechoslovak banks have been allowed by the Eurocheque Community to provide credit cards for Czechoslovak tourists for their trips abroad. Commercial Bank Prague issues those cards for clients with hard currency accounts not only for their trips abroad but also for their shopping in local hard currency stores.

VII

The most important event in the privatization of Czechoslovak banks will be the privatization of state-owned banks carried out under the Act on Large-Scale Privatization (affecting over 600 state-owned enterprises). The privatization will include the two largest commercial banks (Commercial Bank Prague and General Credit Bank Bratislava) and the Zivnostenska Bank Prague, all three of which were founded by the central bank. Also subject to privatization will be the state-owned portion of capital in the Czechoslovak Trade Bank, which is a joint-stock company already and does not need to wait for transformation. Also privatized will be the Investment Bank Prague and the Consolidation Bank Prague, founded by the Federal Finance Ministry, as well as the Slovak Guarantee Bank and the Czech and Slovak Savings Banks, which were founded by the republican finance ministries.

Privatization will be undertaken in two rounds, according to the general timetable approved by the government. It is expected, however, that most banks will be privatized in the second round during the second half of 1992.

Prior to the actual privatization of these banks, an examination of their balance sheets will be undertaken by reputable foreign auditing firms. The banks' property will be newly evaluated and their balance sheets will be cleaned of bad debts. Foreign consulting firms will also assist in finding suitable foreign banks as investors.

Each individual bank prepares a privatization project, which will be reviewed by the founder (i.e., the central bank or the respective finance ministry) and presented to the government for approval. The privatization project determines the amount of shares to be distributed among Czechoslovak citizens in exchange for their investment vouchers (obtained at a token price), the amount of shares to be offered to foreign investors, and the amount of shares for the so-called reprivatization (return of property to former owners).

It is expected that the foreign stake in privatized banks will not exceed 25% (and that of an individual investor 10%) of total capital. Further, 30%–40% of shares should remain as state-owned property in the privatized banks.

So far, the state vouches for the savings of the population in the state-owned banks. As a result of privatization, the state guarantee for savings should be abolished and a Savings and Deposit Insurance Association, financed by commercial banks and the state, should play the role of guarantor.

Another important problem is the role of foreign banks in Czechoslovakia. The present banking legislation does not provide for the establishment of a foreign bank, but, according to another law, it is possible to set up a joint venture bank. At present, there are already seven joint venture banks, which operate jointly with a Czechoslovak bank or alone, for our law on joint ventures permits 100% foreign ownership of banks, which monitor the Czechoslovak market and constitute a nucleus of future foreign subsidiaries.

According to the new legislation, foreign banks will be allowed to establish subsidiaries or joint ventures in the CSFR. It is feared that by allowing the establishment of branches, Czechoslovakia would deprive itself of capital and that the branch would evade supervision by the central bank and gain advantage vis-à-vis the Czechoslovak bank. The license for a foreign bank is issued by the central bank, which places special emphasis on whether the founder can prove a lasting interest in Czechoslovakia's welfare, whether—apart from capital—he or she is bringing in know-how and expertise, and whether the new management has the necessary moral and professional qualities. There is no geopolitical discrimination, yet one is careful to prevent a massive invasion of German banks. There exists no ceiling for the amount of basic capital, which is negotiable, but for the newly established banks the amount of US $10 million is regarded as a minimum. As most foreign bank subsidiaries or joint venture banks are located in Prague, preference will be given to applicants situating their bank in the capital of Slovakia. It is expected that licenses will be issued to about ten new banks in 1992.

So far, the banks are working in the absence of capital and money markets. As a result, the banks are often reluctant to reject a dubious loan, knowing that the fate of the client is entirely in their hands, which induces them to compromises. Such compromises would not be needed if the client could resort to a capital and money market where the soundness of the project would be reexamined. A faster expansion of the capital and money market is, regrettably, discouraged by high interest rates on time deposits, which are tax-free, while dividends on securities are lower and subject to a 25% tax. What is worse, the population suffers from a lack of funds owing to a rigorous wage policy and the decline in the standard of living. The enterprises again give preference to an earlier repayment of expensive bank loans. While some banks look with expectation on the emergence of the market, others fear that the capital market would withdraw resources from them and cut down their lending ability as well as profits. On our market one can find so far only the shares of our foreign trade corporations and about ten issues of tradable bonds, mostly reserved for the issuer's own employees. Only the bonds issued by Commercial Bank Prague and by General Credit Bank Bratislava (each in the value of Kčs 1 billion) are worth mentioning.

A powerful pro-market impulse is expected from a radical transformation of the Czechoslovak insurance system. The prevailing system, which incorporated all types of insurance as integral parts of annual state budgets, has been dismantled, and the newly emerging life insurance funds and pension funds will turn into the vital nucleus of institutional savings. In view of state budget surpluses, envisaged for the forthcoming two to three years, no government papers or bonds are to be expected. Hence, we have to wait until the shares of privatized enterprises become tradable. In the meantime, the necessary legal framework is being prepared. The Law on Bonds has already been enacted, the work on a new commercial code is under way, and the Law on Large Privatization is also in force.

A securities exchange will be established in Prague and Bratislava in 1991. The draft statutes on the securities exchange will be presented to the parliament in mid-1991. The Securities Exchange will have the legal form of a joint-stock company independent of the state, which will only grant licenses and exercise supervision. Trading is reserved only to member banks and specialized institutions. Once business develops, the classic form of the bourse will be replaced by a dematerialized form based on computer entries (as in Denmark). A Preparatory Committee for the Securities Exchange has already been established as a nongovernmental agency registered in the firm's registry and financed under the PHARE program from World Bank funds.

Before the formal establishment of the Securities Exchange, the central bank, jointly with the large commercial banks, had opened (since April 1, 1991) a secondary interim market for bonds. Every two weeks an auction takes place in the central bank at which the market price for bonds is determined by supply and demand. Work is also under way on the preparation of a commodity bourse (particularly for agricultural produce).

4

Monetary and Credit Policy of the National Bank of Poland

PIOTR BOGUSZEWSKI
WŁADYSŁAW CZULNO
WOJCIECH PROKOP

■ *I. Basic Assumptions of the Polish Economic Reform*

The Polish economic reform that began in January 1990 has had three principal goals:

1. curbing the inflationary process quickly and permanently and eliminating shortages of goods on the market;
2. transforming Poland's economic system into a market system;
3. opening the Polish economy, integrating it into the European and world economies.

The stabilization of the economy was a prerequisite to the successful introduction of changes in the economic system. However, without profound changes in the system and the simultaneous introduction of supply-stimulating instruments, economic stability could not pave the way for sustained growth of production, improvement of living standards, and strengthening of Poland's international position in the long term.

Since January 1990, many steps have been taken to curb inflation and to start the transformation of the economy. The main points of the reform package implemented since the beginning of 1990 include:

- liberalization of all prices, except for a few products in heavily monopolized sectors (energy, transport);
- rapid decrease of the budget deficit through cuts in subsidies and other budget expenditures;

Władysław Czulno and Wojciech Prokop are with the National Bank of Poland. Piotr Boguszewski is with the Institute for Banking and Monetary Policy.

- restrictions on wage increases imposed by tax measures that caused significant cuts in real income;
- unification and stabilization of the exchange rate along with the partial convertibility of the domestic currency (now the convertibility is limited to current account operations);
- a consistent anti-inflationary monetary policy, including high interest rates to limit demand for credits and create incentives for increased savings;
- gradual introduction of money and capital market instruments and institutions;
- an active antimonopoly policy, involving promotion of new enterprises;
- changes in the ownership structure through privatization of state-owned firms and enterprises.

In the sphere of foreign trade, all quantitative restrictions on imports from Western countries were removed. Under the new law on investments with participation of foreign capital, all limits on the foreign share in total investments were abolished.

Foreign investors are allowed to buy stock in Polish enterprises or establish 100% foreign-owned firms. In the near future, a new law will be passed that will allow full repatriation of the profits made in Poland by foreign enterprises and banks.

In mid-1990 the parliament adopted a bill on ownership transformation, specifically, the privatization of the economy.

As of mid-1991 the main results of implementing the program were:

- inflation, measured on a monthly basis, dropped from 78.5% in January 1990 to 3.49% in June 1990 and to approximately 0 in July 1991;
- the internal market situation drastically improved, and the relation between supply and demand has balanced;
- in 1990 exports went up by over 20% and imports fell by 20%, creating a huge surplus in the trade balance ($3.8 billion and 4.8 billion rubles), which resulted in an increase in foreign exchange reserves;
- the exchange rate was stable for over 16 months, and there have been no limits on access to foreign exchange by economic entities and the general public.

These promising results have been achieved as a consequence of a fiscal policy aimed at a balanced budget, a restrictive wage policy, and positive interest rates. All these measures and the stable exchange rate have constituted the "anchors" of the stabilization program, but in fact, the real picture is not all that rosy. Some problems remain unsolved. The costs turned out to be beyond the limits of social acceptance, and some remedies have apparently been worse than the disease.

■ II. Dilemmas, Unsolved Problems, and Costs

Despite the serious efforts to implement the stabilization program, not all its goals have been met. First of all, the struggle to curb inflation is still ongoing. Although since March 1990, the average monthly rate of inflation has dropped significantly in comparison with the period of hyperinflation in 1989 and the beginning of 1990, for a long time it remained over the target level of 1% per month. According to pessimistic estimates, the 1991 yearly rate of inflation may even exceed 100%.

The causes of Poland's permanent inflation are the subject of controversy among economists. There is agreement, however, that there are a few factors that explain the situation of permanent inflation.

First, the monetary approach to stabilization has been adopted in Poland. There are, however, several conditions for the effectiveness of such a policy, and some of them have not been satisfied. The stable, or at least predictable, velocity of money seems to be the most important condition of a well-designed monetary policy. Unfortunately, in the second half of the 1980s there was a permanent and sometimes even sharp rise in the velocity of money.

It should be added that those wide variations in the velocity of money are, to some extent, inherent in the period of transition. After the removal of postcommunist prohibitions, new channels of money circulation have been emerging and society has formed new economic habits. It is worth noting that a quick development of the banking and credit system also contributes to the changes of velocity of money. This hypothesis is consistent with the results of recent investigations in developed economies. If this is true, it is confusing for economies such as Poland's. It means that there is a very serious barrier to the implementation of a pure orthodox monetary policy in postcommunist economies.

The second group of problems concerning monetary policy

is connected with the fixed exchange rate regime. Under such a regime, there are difficulties concerning the control of money creation. A huge part of the money supply in Poland in 1990 was a result of the balance of trade surplus, which means that this part of the money creation was practically beyond the control of the central bank, the National Bank of Poland. Now, for many reasons, monetary sterilization is impossible in Poland.

The second shortcoming of the fixed exchange rate regime appears if high domestic inflation is not stopped and the ex post interest rate on zloty-denominated deposits turns out, due to high inflation, to be negative. In such a situation, there are no means of exchange that are able to protect the purchasing power of those deposits. On the one hand, dollar-denominated accounts lose their real value due to simultaneous upward movement of domestic prices and a fixed exchange rate. On the other hand, interest borne on zloty-denominated accounts does not cover the rate of domestic inflation. If we add the absence of a real stock exchange, it is obvious that in Poland there are no rational reasons for keeping financial assets. In the presence of inflation, the absence of a financial hedge against inflation is a side effect of the dedollarization of the economy.

This has very important economic consequences. One is that people prefer trade over investment, or, more generally speaking, over all activities that do not guarantee quick and frequent turnover. In postcommunist economies, this can be called a special mutation of the "crowding out" effect and it refers to the domination of trade over production during the period of transition. Second, in the absence of strong motivation toward holding financial assets, the pace of financial market development is slowed.

These negative consequences of a fixed exchange rate re-gime should be supplemented by two remarks. First, abolishing this regime would cause continuous upward pressure on the exchange rate. We experienced this pressure when we changed the system of exchange rate calculation in June 1991. Second, in a fixed exchange rate regime, the system of extremely diversified interest rates on zloty and dollar accounts plays a very impor-tant role. However, this system, which substantially prefers zloty-denominated accounts and then is effective in stimulating conversion of dollar accounts into zloty-denominated ones, can cause speculative demand for money and, consequently, can destabilize the monetary system in some circumstances. Therefore, it may turn out that resignation from a fixed exchange rate regime is not possible. In that case we will be in a catch-22 situation if sound reasons for abandonment of this regime appear.

The experience at the end of 1990 and the first half of 1991 supports the conclusion that in the very near future, the state's rising budget deficit will probably bring additional problems in controlling the money supply. These problems have many roots. They are partially caused by the excessively restrictive stabilization policy implemented in 1990.

While we were introducing profound changes in the economic system, it was expected that production and consumption would decrease. But the fact is that the decrease is much larger than estimated. Industrial output has decreased by 30%, mainly in consumer goods industries, where production has fallen by 40%. Moreover, despite rising exports in 1990, there was no reason to believe in a long-term extraordinary export capacity of our economy. Then, in the long term, a significant drop in domestic demand would mean the suppression of total demand in our economy. This partially explains the persistence of recession in Poland and the decreasing trend of production under so-called demand-cutting stabilization measures.

The downward trend in industrial production is not the only source of the threat of budgetary collapse in 1991. There is also a second important factor. I have already mentioned that inflation has not been fully eliminated. To be precise, we should say that demand-pull inflation has been constrained but cost-push inflation has not.

In consequence, some distortions in the profitability of enterprises appeared, mainly within the group of state-owned enterprises. The dramatic drop in the rate of profitability in industry since January 1991 means more than just financial problems and the specter of bankruptcy for many firms. First of all, because of a sharp contraction in the tax base, state revenues will decrease. Keep in mind that the main revenue source in Poland is state-owned enterprises. There are two mechanisms activated by worsening profitability of enterprises. If the rate of profitability is low, then not only is the tax base insufficient from the point of view of budget needs, but collection of taxes is also impeded. In 1991 there have been many problems with the collection of taxes. Furthermore, this situation is equally bad for enterprises and leads to a vicious circle. The government, tend-ing toward a balanced budget, tries to impose higher taxes on enterprises, but they are unable to satisfy those claims. Then, outstanding debts of enterprises due to unpaid taxes or, eventually, due to extension of bank credits, rise. (Enterprises in a bad financial position face a trade-off between running into new debts or having overdue repayments.) Finally, the financial standing of those enterprises becomes worse and some of them become insolvent or experience falling rates of profitability. This additionally cuts budgetary income, while simultaneously, budgetary expenditures rise due to increasing unemployment benefits and other forms of government intervention aimed at preventing the threat of massive bankruptcies, massive structural unemployment, social unrest, and so on.

It is clear that in such a delicate social and economic situation, it is very difficult to balance all arguments for and against a balanced budget and to find effective measures for budgetary policy. Despite the very promising results of the first months of 1990, our budget ran a deficit in December 1990 and since then has remained unbalanced. In light of the general economic situation in Poland, especially the very unfavorable prospects for state-owned enterprises, the deep recession in this sector, problems relating to the implementation of the new tax system, and the disastrous financial condition of many institutions belonging to the so-called nonproductive sphere of the economy, there is little chance of finding a simple cure for the budget deficit. Current events confirm this hypothesis: figures for the first half of 1991 are alarming.

A tight monetary policy is one of the most important objectives of the stabilization program. The effectiveness of a pure monetary policy in the period of transition can be limited and is exposed to many constraints. This is confirmed by the experience of 1990 and early 1991 (see table at end of chapter). Bearing in mind the scale of recession in Poland, it is easy to see that the dynamics of money supply do not agree with the so-called fixed growth rate rule. In 1990, the money supply was assumed to be about 41.2 billion zlotys. In fact, the money supply exceeded 100 billion zlotys. By comparing those two figures, we can see the scale of the problems facing monetary authorities in 1990. I would like to emphasize that some of the problems seem unavoidable in the period of transition and, in consequence, the responsibility of the central bank for finding quick solutions should be limited.

As previously mentioned, keeping positive interest rates is one of the most important goals of the stabilization policy. At least two conditions should be satisfied in order to achieve this goal: the "goodwill" of the central bank and the existence of an interest rate formation mechanism that is sensitive to the rate of inflation. Despite many efforts taken up for free credit market creation, in 1990 interest rates in the banking system were strongly correlated to the rediscount rate announced by the central bank. The interest rate policy preferred by the banking system was to set basic interest rates on credits and on long-term deposits slightly above the rediscount rate. Interest on one-year deposits approximated the rediscount rate, while interest on demand deposits was one third of that. It should be stressed that the influence of the international market interest rates was negligible in Poland, due to the residual role of credits allowed in foreign currencies. At the end of 1990, this kind of credit did not exceed 4.5% of total credits. That is why a strong correlation between interest and rediscount rates exists in the Polish system. Under such circumstances, the effectiveness of the positive interest rate policy depends mainly on the ability of the National Bank of Poland to forecast exact inflation rates. Unfortunately, the higher the rates of inflation, the lower their predictability. This explains why, in spite of the determination of the National Bank of Poland, the ex post interest rates can turn out to be below the rate of inflation from time to time. Only market forces are able to create a proper link between interest rates and inflationary expectations. However, we should bear in mind that the Polish economy is still a risky one. In an unstable environment, the development of free interest rates is slow, due mainly to the information gap between debtors and creditors, which can lead to, among other things, the rationing of credit or speculative, hazardous interest rates. The central bank is obliged to fight against this pathology and protect the banking system from the possible negative effects of hazardous interest rate policy conducted by some banks. Then, from time to time, the central bank must intervene in decisions made by some banks; sometimes even in a non-market manner. This intervention slows down the process of implementing the free market interest rate regime. Finally, ending this process usually takes some years and thus, in the meantime, ex post real interest rates can vary between positive and negative positions.

Taking these facts into consideration, one may say that

Poland is now entering the most difficult stage of the implementation of the economic program. We should answer a few basic questions:

- How can economic activity be induced and output growth stimulated?
- How can recession be overcome while maintaining the elements of price and monetary stabilization already achieved?
- How can high economic risk inherent in the transition period be reduced?

■ III. Main Goals of the New Economic Program

At the beginning of 1991, the government presented to parliament an anti-recessionary economic program for 1991–1993. The program, which was approved, focused on:

- restructuring the economy (privatization, support for small enterprises, liberal financial regulations for foreign capital);
- creating incentives for new investments with a modern tax system, which will be introduced January 1, 1992;
- creating a competitive banking system and financial market;
- gradually decontrolling wages to increase their role in signalling appropriate supply and demand responses;
- modernizing the agricultural sector.

The program predicted that the total economic output will increase by 2%–3% in 1991 and by 5%–6% in 1992 and 1993. This output growth rate will require the growth of fixed investment by 12%–15% per year. Higher investments by the government will be directed towards infrastructure modernization, with improved telecommunications being the most pressing need. It is not anticipated that major infrastructure projects will be cofinanced by external sources.

This ambitious investment program will not be successful without serious inflows of foreign capital. They may have different forms:

- credits extended by international financial institutions (IMF, IFC, World Bank, European Bank for Reconstruction and Development);
- commercial credits (guaranteed and nonguaranteed) by Western governments;
- direct investments in foreign-owned enterprises and joint ventures;

- participation of foreign capital in the process of privatization of state-owned enterprises.

To this end, a liberal policy will be pursued towards foreign investment. The government will ensure that its own external borrowing is prudent and will limit guarantees on external debt contracted by state enterprises and public financial institutions to strictly minimum amounts. New external borrowing will continue to be assumed and serviced by the entities benefiting from the borrowed resources.

Monetary policy will be conducted in a manner that restrains the overall expansion of domestic credit to a rate consistent with the inflation objective and the balance of payments target. The basic principle of monetary policy in 1991 is to determine a level of money supply that does not generate inflation while guaranteeing that lack of money does not halt economic processes. The money supply for 1991 was determined on the assumptions of the government's economic policy as well as on the analysis of the National Bank of Poland, which took into account a predicted growth rate of national income, predicted prices of goods and services, the magnitude of the budget deficit, and the amount of foreign currency reserves. It is assumed that the total money supply in 1991 will increase by 45% in comparison to 1990.

We predict that a growing role will be played by domestic currency in comparison to foreign currencies as a proportion of the money supply. Thus, by the end of 1991, domestic currency will constitute 75% of the money supply, whereas by the end of 1990, it constituted only 67%. This tendency is the result of the interest rate policy on deposits in domestic currency. We predict that in 1991, households will increase their bank deposits by 76% and reserves in cash by only 49%. Enterprises are expected to increase their resources in domestic currency by about 60%.

Reserves of foreign currencies will increase by only 10%. The reason for this is the changing situation in the balance of payments. Credits for the population, economic entities, and the budget will increase by 63%. The National Bank of Poland will start issuing bonds. Later, treasury bonds will be issued and the National Bank of Poland will conduct an active policy of obligatory reserves with respect to commercial banks. By doing that, the National Bank of Poland will adjust the liquidity of commercial banks to coincide with the established monetary policy. A rediscount rate and lombard credits will constitute another instrument of monetary policy. In case there is a danger of an excessive supply of money, the National Bank of Poland can introduce temporary quantitative limits on credits.

We will try to determine a rediscount credit rate where rates of interest on credits and deposits will be higher than inflation. The lombard credit rate will be a little higher than the rediscount credit rate. Individual commercial banks will compete to determine the interest rates on deposits and credits. Commercial banks cannot extend credits to economic entities that do not guarantee punctual repayment of credits. Criteria for good credit standing of an economic entity must be strictly obeyed. Preferential credits can be extended only after an agreement with the government that the amount of credit subsidies will be covered by the budget.

The minister of finance and president of the National Bank of Poland will fix a rate of tax-free reserves that will serve as insurance for higher-risk credits connected with the process of structural changes in the economy. By the end of 1993, commercial banks should achieve a capital to assets ratio of 8%. This is the same as most foreign banks.

Very often, small enterprises develop interesting economic initiatives but cannot present sufficient guarantees to receive a credit. In such cases the National Bank of Poland will guarantee commercial banks up to 60% of the difference between the amount of credit and the amount of a guarantee (equity, mortgage).

The exchange rate policy will secure an equilibrium between demand and supply of foreign currencies. In order to secure this equilibrium, the National Bank of Poland may intervene with reserves on currency markets. Finally, in the near future, we will introduce a modern interbank money market. This year a new telecommunication system for the banking network will be in place. Soon, data processing in banks will be completely modernized.

■ IV. Summary

Poland has initiated a program of banking reform in an environment much different from that in other countries of Eastern Europe. The objectives of banking reform are consistent with the objectives of the program of "shock therapy." The macroeconomic situation places great stress on the banking system and the productive sphere of the economy.

It is expected that the macroeconomic situation will continue to improve in 1991. At the same time, institutional and legal changes in the banking system move Poland's monetary system toward the traditional market economy system.

Money supply in the period of transition (million zlotys)

	Cash Circulation	Individual's Savings Deposits	Enterprises' Funds	Foreign Exchange Accounts	Total Supply	Dynamics (previous month =100.0)
Dec. 89	9879.8	8628.9	7841.4	68609.1	94959.2	—
Jan. 90	11105.8	10975.0	15199.0	60012.2	97291.9	102.4
Feb.	14751.2	13583.2	17012.3	57706.1	103052.8	105.9
Mar.	18914.8	16514.2	19719.6	57081.0	112229.6	108.9
April	22093.4	18315.8	22689.5	56660.4	119759.1	106.7
May	22527.9	20294.1	27608.8	56614.6	127045.4	106.0
June	25996.7	22678.3	31420.1	56133.1	136228.2	107.2
July	28344.0	25236.2	37865.4	57198.0	148643.6	109.1
Aug.	30966.4	27577.7	44323.6	58266.9	161134.6	108.4
Sept.	33315.6	29870.9	47282.0	58775.5	169244.0	105.0
Oct.	35450.3	32659.9	49717.0	59252.5	177079.7	104.6
Nov.	38343.5	35712.4	52306.9	59316.7	185679.5	104.8
Dec.	39335.8	40536.8	48372.1	59579.8	188824.6	101.6
Jan. 91	39328.7	45344.8	48009.4	59251.2	191933.5	101.6
Feb.	43459.3	52436.0	46569.7	55775.7	198240.8	103.3

Source: National Bank of Poland

5

Reform of the Banking System in Poland

ANDRZEJ RUDKA

As Poland's economy is quickly becoming market oriented, the banking system, like all other economic institutions in Poland, is undergoing dramatic changes. It was clear even before the recent reform drive that the banking system needed to be reformed. Efforts to introduce limited changes had already been undertaken in the 1980s. But with the formation of a Solidarity-led government in September 1989 and the introduction of a radical program of economic stabilization and restructuring, banking reform became much more urgent. It was obvious that the poorly developed and inefficient banking system would be one of the main obstacles as Poland tried to weather its economic crisis. In the West, financial institutions constitute a critical sector of the economy. This fact has recently been winning more recognition among industrial managers and business executives in Poland, though the pace of change in this respect is still far from satisfactory.

■ *I. Evolution of the System*

A. From the Monobank to a Two-Tier Banking System

Socialist Poland had a strikingly simple financial sector. Despite the existence of four specialized banks, it had, in effect, a monobank system dominated by the National Bank of Poland (NBP), which in 1987 operated 732 bank branches out of a countrywide total of 808 (excluding cooperative banks,

Andrzej Rudka is Senior Research Fellow at the Institute for East-West Security Studies.

associated with one of the bigger units). The NBP's savings bank department monopolized the collection of household deposits. Money or capital markets did not exist, and currency and deposits were the only financial instruments available to households. Enterprises were obligated to conduct all their transactions through one bank account.

This simple and centralized structure was critical to the NBP's role, which was to help implement the central economic plan. It did so by extending credit to enterprises as needed to fulfill their assigned production targets and by guarding against deviations from the central plan.

Banking reform started in earnest in 1982 with legislation elevating the importance of the NBP and monetary policy. Another significant step was the passing of a law in 1982 that allowed enterprises to go bankrupt. This law was to lay the basis for stricter enforcement of credit policy.

At the beginning of 1987, there were four national banks (NBP, PeKaO Co. Bank, the Commercial Bank in Warsaw, and BGZ—the Food Economy Bank) and 1,663 cooperative banks associated with BGZ. Soon, an independent savings bank (State Savings Bank PKO-BP) was created out of the NBP savings department. But that was only the beginning of a general restructuring of the banking sector that was initiated that year.

The first goal of the reform was to transform the monobank system into a two-tier banking system, consisting of the NBP as a full-fledged central bank plus a second tier of independent, profit-oriented commercial banks. Towards this goal, in April 1988 nine state commercial banks were created from the structure of the NBP. In January 1989, the new banks assumed almost all the NBP's commercial credit and deposit operations. Since then, the number of commercial banks has grown steadily, reaching 25 in late 1989, all state-owned except for one. By the end of 1990, there were 75 national banks (commercial, specialized, and others), including 30 in which private capital dominated (plus 104 cooperative banks operating outside the BGZ structure and 1,562 cooperative banks still associated with BGZ). In July 1991, the newly created Union of Polish Banks had 118 members, more than 40 of them private.[1] All of them are free to

---

1. The structure of banking ownership has been quickly changing. In the case of ownership of banks created in 1990, the Treasury's share was 54.5%, that of private capital 13.3% (of physical persons 7.3%), corporate bodies 21.3%,

operate anywhere in the country and with anyone they wish. The NBP is charged with their supervision. In 1990, the first foreign banks started operating in Poland, usually as representative offices (see below).

The NBP law, drastically revised in early 1989 to allow for a full-fledged two-tier banking system, was revised again later in the year to substantially bolster the NBP's independence. As of January 1, 1990, the NBP has had broad powers to execute monetary policy and has no longer been required to submit a detailed credit plan to parliament for approval. Another very important aspect of the revised law is that it severely restricts government borrowing from the NBP, which could undermine the NBP's authority in monetary policy: an upper limit was imposed equal to 2% of budgeted expenditures.

After long consideration, new amendments to the Banking Law were accepted by the parliament in September 1991. Among other things, they strengthened the position of the NBP's president as well as the NBP's supervisory powers over other banks.[2] It is expected that these new rules will further transform the Polish banking system, as—despite considerable changes—it is still far from an efficient, competitive market model.

There are quite a few factors contributing to this situation. First, the supply of banking services is still insufficient in relation to demand, which is rapidly growing, due to institutional changes and the growing role of money in the economy. This allows banks to exercise monopolistic practices and limits the influence of the market on the price and level of banking services. These shortcomings have become particularly evident since mid-1989, when due to the higher inflation rates and institutional changes (a rapid increase in the number of banking accounts), the number of banking operations has been quickly growing.

Second, banking services are still narrow in scope and of low quality. This results from an underdeveloped infrastructure (especially offices, telecommunications, and information sys-

---

and foreign capital 10.9%. If we exclude the Polish Development Bank, the respective shares were as follows: 7.5%, 27.1% (14.0%), 43.3%, and 22.1%.
2. The urgent need for that, as well as for an efficient commercial banking system, was underlined recently by a banking scandal involving a trading company that obtained unsecured credit guarantees from Polish banks and was accused of falsifying documents and bribing bank officials. It also exploited the inadequacies of Poland's banking system by moving checks from account to account faster than the banks were able to notify each other, thus earning interest in several places at the same time.

tems), insufficient competition, shortages of well-trained staff, and lack of specialized financial agents (e.g., in the sphere of housing and agriculture to carry out ownership transformation).

Third, there is a lack of public institutions to support certain specialized banking services, e.g., institutions insuring certain kinds of deposits or the risk connected with certain kinds of credits (export credits, credits for new firms, small and medium-sized producers, etc.).

Fourth, a money market has not yet been developed. The prices for Polish and foreign money, interest rates, and exchange rates are only partly set by supply and demand relations on the money market. The central bank continues to be an important, and in some sectors of the economy (agriculture, construction), prevailing source of credit.

Fifth, in spite of some improvement in 1990, the banks are still financially weak. The average ratio of disposable funds to assets is 1:25, while in the West the proportion is usually 1:12. Besides the dangers this situation poses for monetary and budgetary policies, it also reduces the scale of banking services, curbs innovation, and makes banks increase their margins of profit even to the detriment of the quota of sold services.

The direction and pace of development and modernization of the banking system are aimed at ensuring indispensable conditions for the modernization of the Polish economy, increasing its competitiveness on the world markets, and integrating it into the world economy. As of now, reforms are aimed mainly at speeding up the privatization process in the banking sector, where state banks should be turned into bank stock companies with a prevailing share of private capital.

Privatization of banks has been recently embraced as one of the crucial elements of banking reform in Poland. The first step towards their privatization was made in May 1991, when nine commercial banks were transformed into single-owner (state) partnerships. In June 1991, the decision was made to privatize at least five commercial banks by mid-1992. In autumn of 1991 the first two to be privatized will be Wielkopolski Credit Bank in Poznan and Silesian Bank in Katowice (which, according to Western auditing firms, are the best Polish banks). Both of them have a 12% share in crediting the national economy. The next banks to be privatized are Bank of Industry and Commerce in Krakow, State Credit Bank in Warsaw, and Pomorenian Credit Bank in Szczecin. A Western investment bank (to be chosen in an auction) will help in the privatization of the first banks. It is expected that, after making the final evaluation of a bank, a "strategic investor" will be chosen who will buy a controlling interest of the bank's shares and then manage its functioning. According to Polish privatization experts, there has to be a foreign investor, as no institution in Poland has the experience to do the job properly.

B. Outline of the Polish Banking Sector Model

A universal bank in the form of a stock company, unlimited in regard to the rendered services and the freedom of operation on money and capital markets, will constitute the fundamental element in the model. The majority of shares in the bank will be in the hands of shareholders independent of the state treasury (e.g., individuals, local governments, commercialized state enterprises, and also foreign shareholders).

Universal means that the bank will be licensed to carry out all activities (including investment) provided for in the Banking Law, though consent to carry out some of them may be conditioned on meeting certain requirements. *Unlimited* signifies that while carrying out its operations, the bank will be subject to no limitations other than those ensuing from the principles of a rational economy (i.e., there will be no legal restrictions on the duration of deposits or kinds of securities that banks are allowed to purchase, no limits on participation in enterprises, etc.). The bank will operate on a money market wholly open to banks and partly open to other financial institutions and economic units. It will also be entitled to operate on a capital market on terms no worse than those enjoyed by other participants.

Besides banks, other financial institutions, foundations, investment companies, brokerage firms, and insurance agencies will also operate on markets. Among them will be institutions that administer public means assigned for supporting economic development (e.g., institutions that support the initiation of economic activity, assist enterprises in transitional financial problems, support restructuring processes, carry out public investments, etc.). Most of these tasks will be carried out by a bank network. Some public institutions will be formed to support chosen categories of banking services (e.g., insurance of credits and deposits). In time they all will be privatized.

The needs of socioeconomic development and the necessity to ensure support for government policy require that some banks be specialized, vested with a state mission. In particular there will be banks specialized in keeping public savings (PKO-BP, future Post Bank), state-guaranteed financing of medium- and long-term needs of enterprises, investment projects, restructuring programs (e.g., Export Development Bank Co. in Warsaw, Polish Development Bank Co. in Warsaw, Employees Property Bank Co. in Gdansk, Socioeconomic Initiatives Bank "BIG" in Warsaw), and satisfying financial needs in agriculture (Food Economy Bank-BGZ) and in housing construction (the future Housing Construction Development Bank Co. in Warsaw). Due to the importance of these kinds of financial agents for the development of the country, the process of their formation should be under the supervision of the central bank. On the other hand, six already existing specialized banks still play a predominant role in the allocation of credit, which is not fully consistent with the goal of creating a market allocation system.

Special attention should also be given to cooperative banks, especially in view of the amendments made to the law on cooperatives, which freed such banks from the supervision of the Food Economy Bank. As cooperative banks play an important social and economic function, yet in many cases are very small, special legal regulations should be worked out for them. These regulations should take into account the following: cooperative banks will be registered under general principles, with the capital requirements adjusted to the scope of a bank's activity; cooperative banks will belong to an association of banks or other larger body (e.g., another large cooperative bank).

The National Bank of Poland (the banker's bank) will watch over the functioning of the money market. Its activity will be bound by the legal obligation to protect the value and stability of the domestic currency. The NBP will fulfill this duty in various ways:

- shaping monetary policy and issuing money;
- organizing the money circulation and an accounting system;
- operating a money market and intervening in specific, serious situations;
- controlling bank liquidity by adjusting reserve requirements;

- ensuring the convertibility of the zloty, through, among other things, shaping exchange rates;
- using the state foreign currency reserves for exchange dealings;
- supervising banks to determine whether they are acting wisely with the means at their disposal.

The capital market will be under the control of the Securities Commission, created in the spring of 1991, which includes, among others, NBP representatives. Experts of the US Securities and Exchange Commission helped to create and manage the functioning of that body.

C. Development of the Banking Sector

The implementation of the outlined model calls for numerous measures to be taken. Some of them have already been initiated, some are being launched, while others are beyond the competence of the banking sector.

Formation of a money market is the most urgent task. Its first element was the introduction of short-term banking deposits in the NBP in the first quarter of 1990. The interest on these deposits was settled by tender. The second step is the periodic issue of NBP money coupons, distributed by tender but open to all interested parties. The third measure will be the reduction of the automatic mechanism by which the NBP supplies refinance credits: if banks want to supplement their means, they will have to operate on a money market, which should be conducive to the development of banking services. A stricter discipline in regard to obligatory reserves will be the fourth element, aimed at stimulating demand for overnight credits. The fifth element will be the opening of an interbank market to other parties: the treasury bill will be introduced and a secondary market for it formed; the conditions will be set for the introduction of certificates, bankers' acceptances, and commercial paper.

Following these "central" measures, which should be introduced by the end of 1991, further development of the market will depend on the creativity and activity of banks, and, as in other countries, it is likely to be very rapid. The development and increased activity in the money market should allow market forces to influence the interest rate now set by the central bank. The moment of "marketization" of the NBP's interest rate will also depend on the progress in stabilizing the economy and introducing market mechanisms to other sectors.

Restructuring of the banking system includes:

1. Restructuring the banks' balance sheet to improve their financial standing. Banks will be seriously tried due to the expected bankruptcies of their clients (mainly inefficient industrial enterprises). The experience of other countries shows that banking systems emerge seriously weakened from stabilization programs; hence the task is very urgent. The assets and liabilities of banks, their decision-making procedures, methods for assessing risk, administration systems, etc., will be examined by specialized foreign firms. Results of the research will show the genuine financial standing of banks and will indicate cases where their recapitalization, liquidation, or division will be necessary. The results will also be used to work out medium-term programs for the restructuring of banks. Specific features of banks will be taken into account while working on their restructuring.
2. Commercialization and then privatization of some banks, a process initiated in the first half of 1991. As a rule, the state treasury or state investors will not be allowed to hold a dominant position in bank stock companies. In state banks, which will not undergo privatization, boards of directors will be appointed, composed of outstanding practitioners and scholars, representatives of the Finance Ministry, and possibly other ministries.
3. Restructuring banking services and instruments that the central bank and the Finance Ministry will use to stimulate development of specialized services. The mechanism of insuring credits for private firms that do not have guarantees regularly required by banks is an example of such an instrument. The mechanism has increased possibilities for crediting economic ventures in the private sector. The restructuring of banks is supervised by a commission appointed jointly by the president of the NBP and the finance minister.

Reconstruction of the functions and organization of the central bank has already been initiated. In the first stage, the foreign affairs section was reorganized. This section was involved in introducing the convertibility of the zloty and increasing the intensity of contacts from abroad. Work is under way on the reconstruction of other sections, that is, the treasury-and-issue, operational, economic, and banking sections, the latter being responsible for the functioning and development of the whole banking system. Work has also been undertaken on a new profile of the NBP regional structure. Its aim is to adjust the network of branches and their structure to the changed tasks of the bank.

Separating the function of shaping the bank's strategy, including monetary policy, from the current NBP management will constitute another change. Like other central banks, the NBP should have a board of directors appointed for a definite period (e.g., six to eight years) which would be responsible for, among other things, the principles and directions of monetary policy. It should also have a separate management team to administer current activities of the bank.

The next element is a survey of commercial activity (which includes, among other things, keeping foreign currency accounts for individuals and firms) and the adjustment of its scope to fit the needs of the central bank. Ensuring an efficient monetary policy requires extensive knowledge of economic processes and mechanisms. This entails strengthening the analysis and research section, which will require broader analytical means, new methods, short- and long-term forecasts, and a system to signal threats to the implementation of monetary programs.

Changes will be made in the servicing of the state and local budgets to ensure efficiency and controllability in the processes of shaping budgetary income and expenditure, both at the central and regional levels.

Strengthening of bank supervision has been another prime goal. The General Inspectorate for Bank Supervision, subordinate to the NBP, was set up in 1990. Its task is to ensure the security of banking deposits and the compliance of banks' activity with the provisions of the Banking Law. The supervision is exercised by constant analysis of banks' operations and financial condition and by regular inspections. The following spheres are inspected first and foremost: the adequacy of disposable funds for the pursued credit activity, the quality of assets portfolio and guarantees for credits of doubtful quality by means of adequate reserves, and the degree of competence and caution while undertaking decisions on credits. The strengthening of bank supervision constituted one of the key elements of the 1991 amendments to the Banking Law.

D. Improvement of Banking Services

Critical assessment of the low level of banking services calls for measures that would radically change the quality of banks' work. An interbank team was set up to review all regulations on servicing clients, with a view to restoring the equality of both sides. Unnecessary restrictive and administrative regulations are to be eliminated and the procedure of servicing clients simplified.

The improvement of banks' work will be achieved through the creation of new bank units and the adoption of certain measures in existing banks (i.e., special selection of staff, introduction of the function of inspector-guardian of clients, simplification of banking forms and documents, introduction of foreign currency personal checks or other formulas that would allow clients to use their accounts outside their bank branch, acceptance of personal checks by banks on a reciprocal basis, and initiation of steps towards the elimination of various barriers hindering the development of non-cash turnover).

New bank units will be set up by the purchase or lease of shops (one-, two-, or three-cash desk units), establishment of bank cash desks in department stores and other public buildings (railway stations, hotels, etc.), and agency contracts with selected private foreign exchange desks for performing specific banking tasks.

Implementation of the program to improve banking services will bring about the desired effects, provided there are determined action and substantial means assigned for the purpose. The change in the level of banking services is conditioned on the participation of all banks in the project. Under a new rule, the Council of Banks, with spokespersons for banks' clients and representatives of consumer organizations, will assess banking services on a quarterly basis.

Modernization and development of the banking infrastructure are of critical importance for banking reform. The lack of an efficient communications network in Poland results in, among other things, the disintegration of activity of individual banks; the banks have the character of branch federations rather than coherent bodies.

In view of the necessity to enlarge information systems and the lack of an efficient interbank accounting system, the NBP has launched the construction of a separate communications network, to be composed of two parts. The main network will link 16 regional junctions by fast transmission lines, and the regional one will link bank branches in a given region. The network will cover all of Poland as well as ensure communications abroad. The main lines were to be completed by mid-1991 (recent

COCOM decisions to free most telecommunications technology for export to Poland will be very helpful in creating a modern system in the banking area). In the near future a bank company, Banking Telecommunications Society, which will own and operate the network, will be set up. It is expected that Polish banks, the Polish Post, and specialized foreign partners will be shareholders in the company.

The banking computer system is also being modernized, for a modern bank should be fully automated and operations made instantly. The present situation is far from that ideal; there are numerous branches where computerization has not even been started. Efficient, computerized accounts inside a bank and an easily available telecommunications system provide necessary conditions for the improvement of an interbank accounting system. The target is to make all settlements electronically, but this has not been achieved in any country so far, and Poland is still very far from this goal. An Accounting Chamber that is being set up will ensure that this objective will be reached. Its key element will be the Accounting Center, which will settle accounts among banks using their accounts in the NBP. Documents from the NBP's central office and affiliated accounting centers—regional centers, an electronic accounting center, a telegraphic accounting center, and a check accounting center—will form the basis for settling accounts. The Accounting Chamber should start operations in mid-1991, but a fully electronically operated accounting system is not expected for a few years. Its operation will be conditioned on the development of a general telecommunications system and the pace of computerization in the banks.

The charts of accounts will be remodelled to adjust them to a market economy according to European Community standards. This is extremely important in view of Polish efforts to establish closer economic and financial ties with the EC. The prospect of association with that organization in 1992, with the possibility of joining it at some point, has motivated Poland to move faster in that direction.

Development of competition is badly needed; otherwise, the technical facilities will not have sufficient impact on the improvement of banking services. A liberal policy of licensing new banks is now the major instrument to boost competition. In order to set up a bank, Polish partners have to provide 20 billion zlotys as the statutory capital, prove their good reputation (no criminal record), offer concrete plans for operation, and show some knowledge of banking. There is a considerable interest in setting up new banks. The terms for forming new banks with a share of foreign capital are also generous. The required initial capital of $6 million is probably the lowest in Europe, but foreign banks have shown little interest in setting up banks in Poland so far. Nearly all major banks sought information on the terms of operation in Poland, and a few of them have already taken steps in that direction (see below).

The formation of new banks of various potential and scope of operation will set conditions for improving the efficiency and quality of banking services, lowering their cost, and enriching their variety. It is expected that the growing number of banks and their branches will, in particular, facilitate access to banking services, enable clients to choose a bank freely, improve conditions for servicing clients (especially in regard to foreign currency operations), facilitate the introduction of new banking operations and services, and enlarge the possibilities for developing safekeeping and depositing services.

E. Personnel for the Banking Sector

The process of banking reform calls for the organization of a two-track training system for banking and financial sector staff. The summary training will satisfy the most urgent needs, while a model training program will cover the comprehensive requirements for preparing banking personnel.

Immediate needs are being met by short (two-week) courses and training in foreign banks. The model training program includes restructuring of the economic training profile, with particular stress on the monetary problems and market economy systems in general; organization of an educational structure for the needs of banks, including universities (for example, the Banking University in Katowice), as well as a network of selected economic high schools in large agglomerations; and organization of professional training systems in individual commercial banks. The new model of economic education is to be introduced in the 1991–1992 academic year.

F. Amendment of Legal Regulations

The change of the economic system and the necessity to set conditions for the development of banking services require further deep modifications in legal regulations, both in the laws directly relating to banks and in those defining other spheres of economic life. The most fundamental tasks include:

- Regulation of the principles for forming, licensing, and supervising the activity of non-banking financial institutions. The lack of such regulations results in various units launching deposit and credit activities without legal guarantees for their clients, to the detriment of the banking system.

- Definite settlement of the problem of ownership of property administered by state organizational units and the scope and procedure of dealing with state treasury property. Without a clear solution, it is impossible to properly define creditworthiness, limits, and criteria for assessing banking risk; in the absence of these factors banks are impeded in their operations and foreign relations.

- Determination and agreement on accounting rules in units carrying out economic activity, so that recording and accounting instruments provide an easy and rapid assessment of the economic standing of units that enter into relations with banks; external auditing must also be introduced.

- Specification of legal regulations concerning the proportion in which persons setting up a bank may hold the initial capital. No one should hold more than 50% of the shares and each should be dependent on other partners.

- Definition of the relations between a bank and its founders and shareholders. The rights of founders and shareholders to draw credits and loans should not be greater than the rights of other units.

- Clear authorization that allows the president of the NBP to define capital requirements for setting up a bank and regulations on credit and loan activities.

- Reconstruction of the NBP's financial rules by imposing separate regimes on revenues gained from issuing money (they should be directly related to the state budget) and other kinds of central bank activities (these should be the bank's own revenues, related to the budget only through tax obligations).

- Regulation of the functioning of capital and money markets (organization, operation, guarantees, etc.).

- Adjustment of the regulations on recovery, liquidation, and bankruptcy of a bank to the appropriate foreign rules (among other things, transferring the initiative to recover a bank from its management to a supervising body).

- Adjustment of credit regulations to international standards (among other things, norms on the maximum credits and guarantees, bank credits, and guarantees on credits).

The work on a general restructuring of the Banking Law has already been initiated and was (partially) achieved with the introduction of the new amendments to the Law on the NBP in September 1991. Previous experience and the best patterns of the world banking legislation have been used in that work.

■ *II. Foreign Assistance*

In support of its modernization efforts, the National Bank of Poland turned to, among others, the IMF Central Banking Department (CBD) for technical assistance.[3] The commercial banks had started to develop their market orientation with the assistance of the IMF, the World Bank, and a score of other institutions in 1989. Much is also expected from direct cooperation between Polish and foreign (Western) banks. A large network of such contacts has already been established. Sometimes it is even argued that there are too many different foreign bodies, with occasionally conflicting advice, assisting Poland in building its modern banking system.

A. New Format for Technical Assistance

Traditionally, the IMF Central Banking Department has provided two forms of technical assistance to central banks of member countries: first, sending short-term advisory missions of CBD staff, assisted when necessary by experts of central banks from around the world; and second, assigning central bank experts to the country for a certain period of time. In the case of Poland, the need for assistance was so comprehensive and urgent that these traditional forms were supplemented by a third—securing the direct assistance of a number of Western central banks in the process of modernization of different areas of the NBP's operations.[4]

The work started in late 1989. After familiarizing themselves with the situation and the reform plans already developed

---

3. The following information is based almost exclusively on Anthon A.F. Op de Beke, "IMF Central Banking Department Organizes Aid to National Bank of Poland," *IMF Survey,* August 13, 1990.
4. Ibid., p. 248.

within the NBP, Western experts drafted programs for technical assistance in consultation with CBD staff and later submitted them for approval to the Polish authorities. Since then, the assistance programs have been proceeding in the form of periodic, short-term visits by teams of central bank experts. The CBD has played a coordinating role that involves integrating the technical assistance into broader reform of the monetary and financial system and ensuring consistency across all areas of assistance.

B. Monetary Management and Money Market Development

After earlier CBD advisory missions (in 1988 and 1989), the Bank of England has played, since 1990, a primary role in assisting Poland. With the introduction of the two-tier banking system and the shift of emphasis onto monetary policy, crucial changes in policy framework and its instruments were necessary. The NBP preferred to perform monetary control indirectly rather than exercise inefficient and distortionary direct credit and interest rate controls on banks.

In 1989, the NBP introduced reserve requirements and started to reform its policy for extending refinancing credit to commercial banks. However, "establishing a transparent refinance policy has proven particularly complex owing to the large but unevenly distributed dependence of banks on NBP refinancing. The problem has been compounded by the liquidity problems besetting some of the banks as an outgrowth of the economic reforms."[5] In the same year, the NBP liberalized all interest rates. It now relies on periodic adjustments of its refinance rate to maintain a generally positive (in real terms) interest rate structure. With the abolition of credit ceilings for banks, the refinance rate and the refinance allocations to banks are currently the main monetary instruments employed by the NBP.

The Bank of England has assisted the NBP in several respects:

- Developing "a capacity to translate broad monetary objectives into operational policies and manage bank liquidity with market-

---

5. Ibid., p. 248.

based instruments."[6] The assistance has concentrated on, among other things, measuring, analyzing, and forecasting bank liquidity; and developing market intervention techniques.

- Facilitating monetary management. When the NBP added to its monetary instruments NBP bills that can be used to regulate bank liquidity, the Bank of England experts helped draft the prospectus, the application forms, and other documentation necessary for the auctioning of such bills. The first auction of one-month bills was held in July 1990.

- Promoting an interbank market and a market for bills of exchange, which were reintroduced in Poland in 1989 after a 40-year absence. A strategy has also been designed to gradually develop secondary markets for commercial, NBP, and treasury bills.

C. Monetary and Balance of Payments Research and Analysis

The Netherlands Bank has assisted the NBP in improving its capacity to research and analyze monetary and balance of payment developments. Its experts focused primarily on four objectives:

- Setting up a monitoring system for short-term monetary and exchange rate developments. Information on key variables describing money and credit developments, interest rates, and bank reserves is now collected every ten days from within the NBP and from commercial banks, in the latter case on a sample basis.

- Presenting the information so as to be most conducive to decision making by NBP management. This system has already proven very useful in monitoring the Polish stabilization program.

- Preparing the monthly balance sheet reporting, which constitutes the basis for all banking system monetary data. The classification system has been revised to make it more relevant to current monetary policy making; the distinction between "socialized and nonsocialized" has been replaced by "public and private," the latter subdivided into "households and enterprises" in order to better chart the activities of the fast-growing private sector.[7]

---

6. Ibid., p. 248.
7. Ibid., p. 249.

- Developing the capacity to monitor and analyze, in a timely fashion, balance of payment changes as a factor governing exchange market conditions. This work included improving the balance of payments classification and compilation system and training NBP staff in the Netherlands Bank on these issues and in the computerized processing of massive information flows.

D. Bank Supervision

Bank supervision is a crucial central bank function, since, in addition to disrupting monetary management, even individual bank failures can have serious effects on the public's confidence in the banking system. Experts from the Bank of France have been assisting the NBP in:[8]

- Dealing with commercial risk management, which, owing to the transformation to a market economy with mixed forms of ownership, is entering into banking transactions in Poland. It will also be central to the efforts to modernize the commercial banks, but the NBP can play a leading role by setting proper guidelines.

- Ensuring meaningful and reliable bank reporting, which means changing the plan according to which banks do their accounting. The previously existing system was tailored to monitor fulfillment of the now-abandoned central economic plan and inadequately covered commercial risk. The revision was carried out by French and Dutch experts in close cooperation with Polish commercial banks; the revised plan became effective January 1991.

- Strengthening the solvency and liquidity requirements for banks. This involves drafting regulations concerning, among other things, the treatment of bad loans, credit exposure to individual borrowers and economic sectors, foreign exchange exposure, off-balance-sheet operations, and capital adequacy.

E. Central Bank Accounting

Even as late as 1990, the same accounting plan applied to the NBP and the commercial banks. But as the banks must adopt a plan that reflects their new commercial orientation, the NBP must adopt one that is appropriate to its role as a central bank. Therefore, Austrian National Bank experts

---

8. Ibid., p. 249.

have been helping the NBP with several central bank accounting and internal auditing procedures:[9]

- Adjusting the accounting relationships between the banks and the NBP and for the NBP internally, to a new banking structure in which most previously NBP branches are now commercial bank branches or commercial bank head offices, and only the remainder are NBP district branches.

- Completing centralization of NBP accounts, which was introduced in the fall of 1990 with the installation of a microwave telecommunications network, to which NBP branches and head offices were connected.

- Revising NBP accounting procedures, including the presentation of its balance sheet and profit and loss accounts. For instance, a special reserve was introduced to offset exchange rate-induced changes in the value of foreign assets and liabilities.

- Strengthening the NBP's internal audit function, which at present involves more than verifying compliance with the principles of adequate and orderly accounting and fraud detection; it also involves ensuring the proper conduct, security, and economic efficiency of all operations on the basis of binding rules and objectives.

F. Foreign Exchange Operations

The NBP has had to adapt its foreign exchange operations to two important changes simultaneously: first, the NBP must now manage the country's international reserves, a function that traditionally belonged to the foreign trade bank; and second, it must deal with dramatic changes in foreign exchange policy stemming from liberalization of current account transactions at the beginning of 1990. Experts from the Deutsche Bundesbank have been helping the NBP make adaptations:[10]

- Regarding the NBP reserve management, i.e., strengthening organization, staffing, equipment, analysis of foreign exchange developments, and control procedures.

- Concerning the manner in which exporters surrender foreign exchange proceeds. Currently, banks must surrender all export proceeds immediately to the NBP, while for all import needs,

---

9. Ibid., p. 250.
10. Ibid., p. 250.

they must turn to the NBP. With adequate limits on their open foreign exchange positions, which is a matter for bank supervision, banks could be allowed to play a larger role in the foreign exchange market.

- In the system of foreign exchange controls. Paradoxically, as a result of the liberalization of its foreign exchange regime, Poland had to introduce a system of foreign exchange controls on capital transactions (a fairly loose one that can be easily abolished once the country's external position is strong enough to allow full convertibility of the currency).

G. Payments System

Central banks everywhere carry a responsibility for the smooth functioning of the payments system. Due to historical reasons, the NBP still operates the entire payments system in Poland, including the internal account administration of the commercial banks that were once part of it. With the assistance of experts from the US Federal Reserve System, the NBP has defined a new, more limited role for itself, while at the same time it has promoted drastic modernization of the payments system.

The experts of the Federal Reserve have also advised the NBP in three areas:[11]

- Launching the initiative for a National Clearinghouse (NCH) for small-value payments, which the NBP is now shifting to the commercial banks. The NCH will handle both credit and debit transfers by computer, which will allow elimination of long delays in their settlements.

- Developing a system for the electronic settlement of large-value payments over its own books, as the possibility to settle large-value transactions quickly (preferably on the same day) will be critical to money and securities markets and, by implication, to market-based monetary policy. The NBP cannot continue its unlimited guarantee of the finality of interbank transactions, as it would be exposing itself to serious risks—the commercial banks must manage these risks themselves.

- Improving the safety and efficiency of the current payments system, i.e., centralizing bank branch accounts, streamlining telegraphic transfers, improving the organization of the exchange of paper checks and payment orders, rationalizing current procedures, promoting the use of special "banking

---

11. Ibid., p. 251.

mail" services, and establishing a legal and regulatory structure that ensures efficient payments handling.

H. Privatization

On July 11, 1991, five Western banks (Allied Irish Bank, Instituto Bancario Sao Paolo di Torino, Midland Bank, NMB Postbank from the Netherlands, and Unibank from Denmark) signed agreements (twinnings) with five Polish state commercial banks (those earmarked for privatization). The Western banks agreed to provide long-term technical assistance to help create a modern banking system in Poland. The plan, arranged by the International Finance Corporation, is to be partly financed through the World Bank, which set aside $200 million to provide Western assistance for the modernization and privatization of the Polish banking system. It is expected that eventually all nine commercial banks will be included in such twinning agreements with foreign banks.

■ *III. Foreign Banks in Poland*

In July 1990, the Ministry of Finance issued a notice on foreign bank operations in Poland, stating that, in the view of the Ministry and the NBP, the presence of foreign capital is highly desirable and beneficial for the national economy and for the banking system in particular. By opening branches or wholly-owned subsidiaries and by purchasing shares in new or already established local banks and subsequently developing their business, foreign banks are expected to earn a very attractive return. At the same time, it is expected that they will:

- enable the expansion of Poland's economic relations with other countries;
- facilitate the creation of a financial infrastructure for the inflow of other foreign capital;
- promote growing competition in the banking sector;
- propagate modern bank management methods;
- foster the improvement of banking staff skills;
- expand imports of modern banking techniques in general.

The Banking Law permits involvement by foreigners in the Polish banking system in the following forms: investment by foreigners (up to and including 100%) in new or existing banks constituted as joint-stock companies, and opening of branches or representative offices by foreign banks.

The procedure for establishing a bank in Poland with participation of foreign capital is relatively simple. According to the Banking Law, banks in the form of joint-stock companies, involving foreign persons or foreign shareholders, must be established by at least three legal persons or ten "natural" (physical) persons. Permission to incorporate a bank is given by the president of the NBP in agreement with the minister of finance. The permission to establish a bank may be granted (within 30 days) when the following has been demonstrated: the capital is accumulated for investment, premises and technical facilities necessary to carry out its activities are available, and managerial positions have been entrusted to people with a satisfactory professional background. The posts of president (chairperson), vice presidents, and other members of the bank's board of management should be Polish citizens.

In order to open a branch or a representative office it is necessary to obtain a permit issued by the minister of finance in agreement with the president of the NBP. A representative office cannot perform banking operations, which under the Banking Law are reserved for incorporated banks or branches. The minimum capital in convertible currency brought in by foreign persons must be equal to $6 million or its equivalent in other convertible currencies. The amount in Polish currency contributed by domestic persons is not strictly determined.

Other provisions of the law stipulate the following:

- Banks and foreign bank branches may employ Polish citizens as well as foreigners, provided that foreigners are employed in conformity with relevant regulations.
- They are obliged to perform banking operations in accordance with the Banking Law and other provisions of Polish law.
- They may accept foreign exchange deposits from domestic persons on terms agreed upon in contracts concluded with these persons and taking into consideration all relevant regulations.
- They may retain foreign currency assets abroad up to the level of non-capital liabilities abroad in foreign currency.
- They must maintain foreign exchange reserves at the level determined by the president of the NBP in agreement with the Ministry of Finance.

- They can perform both credit and deposit operations in zlotys and in other currencies based on the same conditions applied to domestic banks, i.e., the conditions are freely negotiable. The state treasury is not responsible for a bank's liabilities with respect to deposits from domestic persons, including the saving deposits of individuals; however, it may choose to grant a guarantee or a warranty for such liabilities.
- They must maintain an obligatory zloty reserve with the NBP in accordance with requirements for domestic banks.
- They are required to pay taxes according to principles and rates applying to domestic banks; the profit of a bank after taxation will be constituted by its distributable earnings.
- They should conform to interbank and other settlement practices in the Polish market, prepare their accounts in line with Polish practices and regulations as they apply, and from time to time prepare and submit to the NBP such information and data as domestic banks may be required to submit.
- They are required to carry on correspondence with Polish state offices in the Polish language.
- In general, they are subject to monitoring by Polish financial authorities and specifically to banking supervision exercised by the NBP.

The Ministry of Finance and the NBP agree to treat all banks, foreign and local, equally; however, certain universally applicable practices will be formulated in specific areas. So in the interest of clarity and of equal treatment of all foreign banks, the following guidelines have been laid down:

- New banks must maintain capital at no less than 8% of weighted risk exposure. Polish regulations in this area are to be further refined and will conform to BIS and EC Directive methodologies.
- Banks may maintain their capital (including accruals) in foreign currencies on account with the NBP on conditions negotiated with the NBP.
- Capital revalued in zloty terms due to foreign exchange movements will not incur a tax; by the same token, losses will not be deductible.
- There is free transfer abroad in foreign currency of the originally imported capital plus capital gain, if any, on the disposal of any or all of the shareholding or branch capital in a bank. Such transfer will be subject to normal administrative supervi-

sion by the NBP and will be possible after deduction of any applicable Polish taxes.

- The remittance in foreign currency of at least 30% of remittance profits is permitted; larger percentages require acceptance by the NBP.

- Equipment imported for banks, as in the case of other foreign investors, would be free from duty for three years from original establishment.

- Foreign employees of banks are expected to be subject to applicable Polish tax; there is no duty on personal goods brought in by such employees.

- Banks may acquire property freely from private individuals. In regard to state land and real estate, currently applicable Polish law permits long-term rental (up to 99 years) or, in certain circumstances, purchase with the permission of the minister of the interior; joint-stock banks formed with Polish shareholders may have real estate contributed as or towards the Polish shareholder's subscription.

- The NBP will favorably consider applications from banks for refinancing lines in zlotys in order to obviate any difficulties at this stage in the development of the interbank market. This will normally be in the form of a rediscount facility which will be at interest terms no worse than the NBP offers to other banks of similar standing; the size of the line will be resolved by bilateral discussion.

- With respect to the policy of reserves covering bad debts of banks, it is accepted as an interim solution that banks will be able to gather reserves at the level of 1% of credit liabilities at the end of every quarter and the total annual amount of reserves will be at most 5% of credit liabilities; all of these would be deductible for tax purposes.

- The Banking Law states that the volume of credits granted to one borrower or group of borrowers cannot exceed 15% of the total of paid-in capital (excluding retained earnings and other reserve accounts if any) plus deposits.

Foreign banks have usually started their cooperation with Poland with the creation of representative offices, not operational branches, which is a sign of their cautiousness in entering a country that is still economically and politically unstable. So it is understandable that before starting full-fledged financial operations in Poland, they prefer to observe the market, gather experience, and establish a network of business contacts. Later on they can transform their representative offices into operational branches, as has been the case with many foreign industrial firms, which, after a period of waiting, entered into joint ventures with Polish enterprises.

There are, however, other reasons for the relatively small activity of foreign banks in Poland so far, e.g., possibilities for investment in other East European countries, Poland's indebtedness, refusal to accept Polish promissory notes as a whole or a part of contribution to the capital of a bank, etc. In order to boost interest in setting up foreign banks in Poland, it is proposed to introduce similar taxation solutions for them as for other joint ventures and to liberalize the principles of profit transfer.

■ *IV. Summary*

The lack of a developed, modern banking system is one of the biggest obstacles to the success of economic reform in Poland, especially to its second and more difficult phase, i.e., the restructuring of the economy, with the emphasis on privatization. This fact has been increasingly recognized by Polish economists and politicians. This awareness of the importance of the banking sector helps to strengthen their resolve to reform that sector as soon as possible.

The efforts in that respect, undertaken with the valuable assistance of international financial institutions and the banking community, have concentrated on a few critical areas:

- developing a Western-style two-tier banking system, consisting of a strong, independent central bank with regulatory control over a network of competitive commercial and other banks;
- bringing Polish banking law and accounting practices into conformity with world standards, especially those of the European Community, with which Poland will be associated as of 1992;
- privatizing state-owned banks and encouraging the creation of privately held banks;
- attracting foreign banks to the Polish financial markets.

The emergence of a new banking system has been a difficult and sometimes painful process, not without a few financial scandals and frauds. The strong commitment to push financial reforms irrespective of those problems bodes fairly well for the Polish banking community's expectations that an effective banking system will be implemented within the next few years.

NOTE ON SOURCES

This paper is based on numerous Polish materials, including those of the banks (most of them unpublished) and information taken from various Polish and foreign journals and newspapers. It is supplemented by information published in:

Act on the Narodowy Bank Polski of January 31, 1989, as amended on December 28, 1989.

Banking Law of January 31, 1989, as amended on December 28, 1989.

Blattman, Rupert. "Socialist Banking System on the Road to the Market Economy," in *Economic and Financial Prospects*, 1990, no. 6 (Swiss Bank Corporation publication).

Building Free Market Economies in Central and Eastern Europe: Challenges and Realities (Washington, DC: The Institute of International Finance, 1990).

Foreign Exchange Law of February 15, 1989, as amended on December 28, 1989.

Law on Companies with Foreign Participation of June 14, 1991.

Op de Beke, Anton A.F. "IMF Central Banking Department Organizes Aid to National Bank of Poland," *IMF Survey*, August 13, 1990.

LIST OF MAIN BANKS IN POLAND AS OF MID-1991

Main Polish Banks (year of foundation)

Central Bank
Narodowy Bank Polski (National Bank of Poland), Warsaw (1945)

Nine Commercial Banks (all created in 1989)
Bank Depozytowo-Kredytowy (Deposit and Credit Bank), Lublin
Bank Gdanski (Gdansk Bank), Gdansk
Bank Poznanski (Poznan Bank), Poznan
Bank Przemyslowo-Handlowy (Industrial and Commercial Bank), Krakow
Bank Slaski (Silesian Bank), Katowice
Bank Zachodni (Western Bank), Wroclaw
Komunalny Bank S.A. (Community Bank, Inc.), Bydgoszcz
Panstwowy Bank Kredytowy (State Credit Bank), Warsaw
Pomorski Bank Kredytowy (Pomeranian Credit Bank), Szczecin

Specialized and Other Banks
Agrobank (Agricultural Bank), Warsaw
Amerbank (American Bank in Poland, Inc), Warsaw (1990)
Bank Gospodarki Zywnosciowej (Food Economy Bank), Warsaw (1975)
Bank Gospodarstwa Krajowego (National Economy Bank), Warsaw (1989)

Bank Handlowo-Kredytowy S.A. (Commercial and Credit Bank of Katowice), Katowice (1990)

Bank Handlowy S.A. (Commercial Bank, Inc.), Warsaw (1870)

Bank Inicjatyw Gospodarczych (Economic Initiative Bank, Inc.), Warsaw (1989)

Bank Polska Kasa Opieki S.A. (Bank Pekao, Inc.), Warsaw (1929)

Bank Rozwoju Eksportu S.A. (Export Development Bank), Warsaw (1987)

Lodzki Bank Rozwoju (Development Bank in Lodz, Inc.), Lodz (1990)

Market SA (Bank for Development of Craftsmanship, Trade and Industry), Poznan (1990)

Polski Bank Rozwoju (Polish Development Bank), Warsaw (1990)

Powszechna Kasa Oszczednosci—Bank Panstwowy (State Savings Bank), Warsaw (1986)

Powszechny Bank Gospodarczy (General Economic Bank), Lodz

Prosper Bank, Inc., Krakow

Wielkopolski Bank Kredytowy (Credit Bank of Wielkopolska), Poznan

Main Foreign Branches of Polish Banks

Bank Handlowy, Inc., Representative Office, London, U.K. (branch)

Bank Handlowy, Inc., Predstavnik Beograd, Belgrade (foreign office)

Bank Handlowy, New York (foreign office)

Bank Handlowy has also shares in the following banks:

Commercial Bank International, Luxembourg

Mitteleuropaische Handelsbank AG, Frankfurt-am-Main (70% Bank Handlowy and 30% Hessische Landesbank-Girozentral, Frankfurt)

Centro International Handelsbank AG, Vienna (Bank Handlowy holds 1/7 of the capital)

Bank Polska Kasa Opieki has three foreign branches: in New York, Paris, and Tel Aviv and has shares in 2 foreign banks mentioned above (in Luxembourg and Frankfurt-am-Main)

Foreign Banks in Poland (usually representative offices)

Banca Commerciale Italiana (Milan), Warsaw (office since 1974)

Bank Nationale de Paris, Warsaw

Centro Internationale et Commercial, Warsaw

Centro-Internationale Handelsbank AG (Vienna, 25% shares of NBP), Warsaw (office since 1985)

Citibank Poland, S.A. (New York), Warsaw (office since 1990, operations since 1991)

Credit Industriel et Commercial de Paris Banque de l'Union Europeenne, Warsaw (office since 1975)

Deutsche Bank AG (Frankfurt-am-Main), Warsaw (office since 1989)

Dresdner Bank AG (Frankfurt-am-Main), Warsaw (office since 1989)

Mittel-Europaeische Handelsbank AG (Germany)

NMB Postbank (Netherlands), Warsaw (1991)
PEKAO Trading Corporation (New York), Warsaw (office since 1988)
Privatbanken AS (Denmark), Warsaw (1990)
Skandinavska Enskilda Banken, Warsaw (1991)
Societe Generale (Paris), Warsaw (office since 1976)
Union Bank of Finland, Warsaw (1991)

6

Money, Banking, and Credit: The Case of Bulgaria

MILETI MLADENOV

■ *I. Introduction and Macroeconomic Overview*

At the end of 1989, Bulgaria began a transition from a 45-year-long totalitarian communist rule to a democratic society whose main feature is the market economy. The initial changes have been peaceful. The country now has a multiparty political system. For the first time in 45 years, a freely and democratically elected parliament is functioning. Its mandate is limited in time—after the new constitution is adopted, it will be dissolved. The Socialist (formerly Communist) Party currently has a simple majority in parliament. At the same time there is a powerful opposition. According to the prevailing public opinion and sociological research, the next elections will change the proportion of the political forces represented in parliament. Expectations are that the present opposition parties will be in the majority.[1]

Ever since November 1989, significant changes have been taking place in Bulgaria. These changes give reason to conclude that Bulgaria is no longer a totalitarian communist country, regardless of the Socialist Party's present majority in parliament. Important changes have been made in the existing constitution: the right to private ownership has been restored, and the state monopoly over foreign trade, banking, etc., has been done away with. Limitations over the right to citizenship in the cities have been abolished, and the foreign exchange regime has been

---

Mileti Mladenov is Deputy Governor of the Bulgarian National Bank.
1. Recent elections have brought the opposition parties into control of the parliament, as the author predicted.—Eds.

liberalized. Some laws have been amended, and new ones have been adopted, including the law on land ownership, the law on accounting, the trade code, the law on foreign investments, and the law on central banking. Adoption of the law on privatization, the law on commercial banking, and some other laws concerning economic activity is pending.

The true, radical changes in the economy began in February 1991, when prices on about 90% of all products were liberalized, the central bank's basic interest rate was increased to 45%, a foreign exchange market with floating rates of currencies was introduced, and wage increases were restricted.[2]

Since the end of 1989 the country has been in a deep economic crisis. The main reason for this is the cumulative effect of the contradictions and problems in the course of the 45-year-long communist rule. Their manifestation is the general imbalance of the national economy, the great commodities shortage, a monetary overhang, large budget deficits, and the enormous (compared to the size of the economy) foreign debt. The old economic structures began to disintegrate at the end of 1989, but there are no new ones to take their place. Bulgaria, unlike other East European countries, was strongly connected to CMEA and the USSR in particular, a fact that in the past did not stimulate effective production, quality, or rational and advantageous trade. The Persian Gulf war also exercised a negative influence over the national economy, as local production is strongly dependent on oil imports. An expression of the economic crisis is the drop in production measured in constant price GDP. Production dropped by 1.9% in 1989, by 12% in 1990, and by 17.5% in the first quarter of 1991. Output in industry in 1990 decreased by more than 20% and in agriculture by 15%. This decrease in production is still continuing. It is expected that the total drop in production for all of 1991 will be about 20%. This is the main problem for the country in the short run. It is considered that the drop in production cannot be stopped before the end of 1991. This is not an easy problem, because national production is strongly dependent on imports of raw materials, while the structural transformation of the economy is only at its initial stage and will, to a great extent, depend on the pace of privatization and foreign financial assistance.

---

2. Statistical data presented in this paper are from the Annual Report of the Bulgarian National Bank, 1990.

Investments were cut in 1990. Unemployment now amounts to 4% of the working population, and the expectation is for its sharp growth (up to 10%) because of the start of privatization, the closing down of unprofitable enterprises, demonopolization, and the expected foreign competition. Because of the great commodities shortage, a system of rationing was introduced in 1990, but it was removed in the beginning of 1991, as almost all prices were liberalized.

The commodities shortage and the amounts of savings of the population called forth a considerable increase of prices, particularly at the beginning of 1991. A reasonable measure of inflation is the index of consumer prices, calculated on the basis of a "basket" of 1,500 goods and 200 services. In the period of May-December 1990, when systematic observations were made, this index grew by 50.6%. For the first months of 1991 the rate of inflation was:

January:	13.6%
February:	120.9%
March:	50.5%
April:	5.5%
May:	0.76%
June:	5.9%

The jump in consumer prices in February 1991 is due to the almost full liberalization of prices at the beginning of that month. Only the prices of some products (oil, electricity, and power) were fixed by the state, but in June these were also liberalized, within some upper limits fixed by the government. The actual increase in prices of basic foodstuffs and some industrial goods and services is much greater than the consumer price index and amounts to a four- or fivefold increase. It is significant that after the initial "price shock" of February 1991, a decrease in some prices was observed and is still continuing. Most economists consider the February price jump a means of price adjustment, as this was the first ever total liberalization of prices. They forecast minor inflation till the end of the year. The reason for these expectations is the elimination of the money overhang, accompanied by a 40%–50% drop in consumption, as well as the restrictive monetary and fiscal policy. At the same time, though, there are opposite fears of some growth of inflation. These fears are caused by delays in privatization, softening of the limitations on wage growth, and a relaxation in the restrictive character of monetary policy.

There are great deficits in the state budget. The cumulative deficit in the budget was 17 billion leva by the end of 1990. For 1990 alone, the deficit was 3 billion leva, which is 13% of GDP. The expected deficit for 1991 is 6.8 billion leva. So far this debt has been financed directly by loans mainly from the National (central) Bank and the State Savings Bank. It was only at the end of 1990 that the first government bonds were issued, with a term of one year and effective interest rate of 44%. An issue of new regular short-term treasury bills will begin in mid-1991. Until now, budget deficits have been one of the main factors of inflation; therefore, a policy of considerable reduction of budget expenditures has been adopted.

The state of the balance of payments is unfavorable: the deficit in the balance of payments for 1990 was US $860 million to the countries with convertible currencies, and 870 million transferable rubles to the CMEA countries. In 1990, exports decreased by 20% in convertible currency and by 42% in transferable rubles. The drop in imports in 1990 was 29% and 12% respectively. The tendency of both imports and exports to decrease began in 1988 and has continued through the beginning of 1991, when the estimates are for a dramatic twofold drop in exports.

Bulgaria has a huge foreign debt, which grew after 1980 and 1985 in particular. The total amount of the gross foreign debt in convertible currency reached US $11.2 billion in 1990. Because of difficulties in servicing the debt, the government imposed a moratorium on payments on both capital and interest in March 1990. This had very serious and still ongoing negative consequences for the prestige of the country. In the meantime, negotiations with creditors are being held on the issue of debt rescheduling and settlement. Talks with the official creditors (the Paris Club) are at a more advanced stage than those with the private creditors (the London Club). The larger part of the debt (about 90%) is to private creditors. The unsettled problems with the debt are an obstacle to the flow of "fresh" money into the country, and it cannot be fully compensated for by credits from the IMF, the World Bank, the European Community, or some other sources.

Financing from abroad so far comes only from the IMF. Bulgaria has been a full member of the IMF since September 25, 1990. On February 25, 1991, the IMF, under the Compensatory and Contingency Financing Facility, adopted an amount of 60.6

million Special Drawing Rights as compensation for the rise in oil prices after the Persian Gulf crisis. On March 15, 1991, an agreement was signed for a standby arrangement for 279 million Special Drawing Rights for 12 months from which the first tranche was in the amount of 77.5 million SDR. Continuing talks are under way with the World Bank and the European Community for additional structural adjustment loans.

■ II. Monetary Policy

Monetary policy, particularly since the beginning of 1991, is strongly restrictive. A limited number of tools are being used. Minimum reserve requirements have been introduced on deposits with commercial banks. Until December 1990 reserve requirements were 5%, and since then 7%. These are interest-free reserves, calculated on the total amount of deposits. Credit ceilings are also in force. In 1991 ceilings were initially fixed at 102% of the credit issued by the respective commercial bank at the end of the previous year; later the ceilings were increased to 109% and 112%.

The main instrument of monetary policy is now the interest rate at which commercial banks are refinanced by the central bank, because commercial banks do not have enough resources of their own. In 1990 this so-called basic interest rate was 4.5%. The interest rate on demand deposits was fixed at 1% in 1990, and on term deposits at 3%. That same year, the average interest rate on bank credits was 5.21%. Interest rate levels up until the beginning of 1991 were very low and practically did not play any economic role. On January 8, 1991, the basic interest rate was raised to 15%, in February to 45% and in June to 52%; in the beginning of July it was decreased to 47%. Interest rates on deposits and credits are negotiated between banks and their clients, except interest on old loans of the public, which were regulated with a special law. Thus, the old system of fixed interest rates was dropped and floating interest rates were introduced.

For a country undergoing a period of transition, the interest rate is something more than an instrument of monetary policy. It is one of the main "anchors" of the economy, along with the restrictions over wages in the state sector. The high level of interest rates and the limiting of wages curtailed demand at a time when prices and the foreign exchange rate were liberalized. This has had its effect because, if we exclude the initial jump in prices, the consequent increase of prices is insignificant. High interest rates directed part of the "excess" money to time deposits, thus absorbing part of the demand of commodities and foreign exchange as well.

Prior to February 19, 1991, there was an official exchange rate of the local currency against foreign currencies, and the exchange rate of the latter was very low. Besides that, there were foreign exchange coefficients, which created a number of exchange rates. At the initiative of the Bulgarian National Bank (BNB), an interbank foreign exchange market was established on February 19, 1991, thus introducing a uniform exchange rate of the leva. This is a floating rate based on demand and supply of foreign exchange within the framework of individual banks and among banks too. The BNB can intervene on the foreign exchange market. Initially the exchange rate of the leva was very low, but it later began to rise, and since mid-April 1991 it has remained at a level of 16–18.50 leva against US $1 with minimum or no intervention on the part of the BNB in the last months. This rate is comparatively unfavorable for importers, but the country has no foreign exchange reserves to finance imports.

In 1988, 1989, and 1990, the money aggregate M2 was larger in volume than the GDP in current prices. In 1990, M2 grew by 18.5%, and M1 by 31%. The results of the restrictive monetary policy this year are expected to slow the growth in these aggregates.

The country's monetary policy has a clear anti-inflationary direction. The wish and objectives of the government are also to control inflation in the very difficult first months of the transition to a market-oriented economy that began in February 1991. As market structures, including those in the financial sector, are just coming into existence, the central bank is not able to use the typical instruments of monetary policy to full advantage. These monetary instruments—for instance, the issuing of state treasury bills—will become the basis for open market operations. There is no possibility for discount operations yet, as commercial paper is practically not used.

■ III. The Banking Sector

Until 1987, Bulgaria's banking system resembled the banking systems of the other East European countries. It was a monobank system in which the national bank performed through its branches and subsidiaries the functions of a universal bank—both commercial and issuing currency. In 1987 and 1990, commercial banks were established. Some of these banks specialized in several branches of the economy and most of the remaining were reorganized BNB branches. Besides the commercial banks, there is a well-developed network of the State Savings Bank (SSB), which has over 2,500 agencies, including the post offices. The total number of people employed in the banking system, including the SSB, is about 18,000. The saturation of bank services from the viewpoint of the banking network, as well as the number of people employed, is far below European and world standards.

Although legislation allows commercial banks to perform universal operations, these banks are not independent. They are set up as shareholdings, but their owners are state enterprises and the BNB. In most of the banks the BNB's share participation is quite large. Only a small number of these banks have their own capital in significant amounts. Only seven banks have equity above 100 million leva (equivalent to US $5.6 million at the current exchange rate of US $1 to 18.00 leva); 28 commercial banks have equity below 10 million leva (US $0.6 million). Most of these banks are regional, and only 11 have full licenses for foreign exchange operations. The resources of the system of commercial banks as a whole are provided mainly by the BNB, which on its part collects them from the SSB and the State Insurance Institute. Thus, the population, the main net creditor, keeps deposits with the SSB, while enterprises, the main net debtor, receive credits from the commercial banks. The BNB plays the part of intermediary in the movement of savings. The lack of their own deposit base, along with the irrational movement of free money resources, is one of the important problems for the commercial banks. The BNB is trying to limit the mechanism by which commercial banks are refinanced automatically. For instance, since January 1991, it has provided only up to 20% of the resources needed by the commercial banks for long-term credits, and this is done in the form of deposits the BNB keeps with the commercial banks.

It is obvious that throughout the country there are too many banks without sufficient equity and hence without chances of developing and surviving under competition. It is necessary to merge some of them. This is possible because the main owners are the central bank and the state (here of course the few private commercial banks are excluded). In the long run, commercial banks will be gradually privatized, including through foreign participation in their equity. The government and specialists are well aware that without the sound health of the commercial banking sector, the irrational distribution of money resources will continue, thus hindering the successful pace of economic reform.

The central bank has a particularly significant role to play in the process of the banking system reform, as well as in implementing economic reform. The BNB, until recently a subsidiary of the State Planning Committee and the Ministry of Finance, will gradually turn into a central bank. The law on the BNB has now been adopted by parliament. The BNB is an autonomous institution directly subordinated to parliament and not to the government. This makes it possible for the BNB to be a partner of the government in carrying out its economic policy.

Active work has been accomplished in the BNB to transform it into a typical central bank. To this purpose technical assistance is rendered by the IMF's Central Banking Department. So far three missions of this department have visited Bulgaria. The joint work continues.

▮ *IV. Ownership in Commercial Banks*

In the period after World War II there existed several specialized banks in Bulgaria. Among them of primary importance were the Bulgarian Foreign Trade Bank and the State Savings Bank, which specialized in transactions with both foreign banks and the population. They still exist today, but are state-owned.

In 1987 the first commercial banks, eight in number, were set up. They specialized in investment operations (long-term credits) for specific branches of industry. Short-term crediting of all branches was carried out through BNB subsidiaries. The new specialized banks are set up as shareholding companies. State enterprises are shareholders, and because of this, the new banks are still essentially state-owned. Mostly state firms keep their deposits in these banks. The deposits are not explicitly guaranteed (insured) by the state. They can, however, be considered indirectly state guaranteed, as the state is the actual owner of the banks.

The establishment of commercial banks in 1987 was an attempt to decentralize the banking system. But banks remained state property, they were only specialized in long-term credits, and they were not autonomous, as they were refinanced on a large scale by the central bank. That is, both in form of ownership and in character of operations, they can be considered a variation of a monobank system and not a radical change towards a two-tier system characteristic of developed countries.

A more serious attempt at a transition to a two-tier system was made in 1990, when the BNB branches and subsidiaries, 59 in total, were administratively reorganized into independent banking institutions called commercial banks, with a juridical status of shareholding companies. With a few exceptions, state firms are still the principal shareholders. Most of these banks have a strong regional character. They have no network of subsidiaries, their own capital is small, and the deposits kept with them are insignificant in amount. The central bank owns more than 50% of the share capital in about one-third of them, and continues to refinance them on a large scale.

As of July 1991 there were 70 banks in total in Bulgaria: they include the Bulgarian Foreign Trade Bank, the Agricultural Credit Bank, the First Private Bank, eight former specialized banks, and 59 commercial banks established on the basis of ex-BNB subsidiaries. The banking system also includes the State Savings Bank, whose activity is regulated by a separate law. The SSB is wholly owned by the state; it is an independent juridical person but is subordinated to the BNB. Although they are universal from a juridical point of view, in fact banks throughout the country differ greatly in their financial capacities. The former BNB branches have limited licenses for foreign exchange operations. Today the banking sector is dominated by the former specialized banks that have significant amounts of their own capital and a relatively small BNB share in their capital, and that have subsidiaries throughout the country. Only the First Private Bank, set up as a private bank, is privately owned. Two more commercial banks have prevailingly privately owned capital (above 50%). All other banks are in practice state property, which raises the question of their privatization. Naturally, in the banking sector in the developed countries there also are state commercial banks, but private banks usually dominate there.

The privatization of the commercial banks means fulfilling the banking reform and completely building up the two tiers in the banking system. Only on the basis of privatization can commercial banks achieve real economic autonomy, which in turn is the prerequisite for stabilizing the banking sector. Where state ownership predominates, there is no foundation for real decentralization and differentiation of banks as merchants of money who bear the risk in their transactions. At present the state, the indirect owner, is behind the commercial banks. The commercial banks have not been completely detached from the state and the BNB. This hampers their development as true commercial banks. In most cases commercial bank transactions are aimed at providing credits for shareholders, which brings about distortions in their activities, as the bank expresses the interests both of the owner and the depositors. Another problem connected with the issue of ownership is the large number of doubtful and often uncollectible receipts of commercial banks from state enterprises, which are now the owners of the bank.

The problem of restructuring the system of commercial banks is also being discussed. By merging banks, the aim is to reduce their number and make them more stable, with a developed network of subsidiaries, with their own deposit base, and competitive under conditions of foreign competition. This restructuring could be implemented within the framework of a bank holding or a consolidating bank, as is suggested by some foreign experts (similar to the project in Czechoslovakia). This would open up the road to privatization of the banks. The SSB, a state bank servicing the population, but also a bank with growing universality of operations, is included in the restructuring project.

■ V. Asset Management in Commercial Banks

Given the present situation of state commercial banks, it is difficult to speak of managing their assets in compliance with world standards and principles. In this connection several problems exist. On the one hand, an obstacle to the real management of assets that could solve the dilemma of "liquidity versus profit" is the lack of full differentiation of banks on the basis of private ownership. Banks are operated first and foremost according to the interests of the owners—the state firms who are interested in receiving credits from them under favorable terms. On the other hand, the BNB, as the largest shareholder in most of the banks, provides resources at the basic interest rate, thus guaranteeing not only the liquidity for central bank refinancing, but also creating the possibility that these resources will form a considerable part of the commercial banks' profits.

Most of the commercial banks and more specifically the former specialized banks have a considerable number of bad loans to state enterprises. These loans existed before the banks were set up and were transferred to them from the BNB in the process of their establishment as independent banks. These bad loans are not a result of the activity of the banks, nor a result of careless operations and poor asset management by the commercial banks. In the centrally planned economy, state bodies directly ordered both the allocation of the amounts of credits and the recipient of the credits. The material form of bad loans is either long ago spent ("eaten up") or has been used for real capital investments that are unprofitable, incomplete, or not in operation.

This problem is being discussed now on the basis of the government's analysis and assessments of the situation in state enterprises, as well as in connection with privatization. The most probable solution is the replacement of the commercial banks' bad loans with long-term state securities and a gradual repayment of these loans from several sources, such as interest on the state securities and revenues from privatization and the probable sale of creditors' property. It is thought that it will be possible to clean up the balance sheets of the banks, and thus a solid foundation will be laid for improving the quality of their credit portfolios. This problem must naturally be solved in conjunction with the restructuring of the banking system, as individual banks find themselves in different situations regarding bad loans.

Together with the real differentiation of the commercial banks and their privatization, it will be possible to advance toward management of assets in the traditional sense, which, of course, is one of the main aspects of commercial banking. The state ownership of commercial banks and the large number of bad loans are the millstones weighing down the commercial banks and distorting their attempts at autonomous asset management, which, in turn, would bring commercial banking into harmony with the principles of profit, liquidity, and security.

Finally, according to the legislation enacted and the draft law on commercial banking, banks will maintain ratios determined by the central bank that are liable to periodic control and sanctions. Through these ratios, which are common world practice, it is considered that the minimum stability of banks will be ensured.

■ VI. The Role of Foreign Capital

Foreign capital could play an important role in strengthening and developing the country's banking sector. Unfortunately, foreign banks have shown little interest so far in launching operations here. A probable explanation for this lack of interest is the huge foreign debt to private and official foreign creditors. This is a result of a unilateral moratorium on debt repayment declared in 1990 by the former communist government. Until recently an additional obstacle was the lack of clear laws on foreign investment, although some laws have already been adopted by parliament, and the passing of several other laws is pending very soon.

The part to be played by foreign capital could consist of setting up subsidiaries of foreign banks as well as joint banks. Applications for establishing joint banks or foreign subsidiaries have been examined. It is assumed that with Bulgaria's advance along the road to democratization, trust in the country and in national banking will grow.

The channels of foreign capital penetration and the use of foreign experience have been established through cooperation with the IMF, the World Bank group, the European Community, and the European Bank for Reconstruction and Development. A mechanism has been created for using foreign resources, to ensure their effective placement and repayment. The BNB and the commercial banks play a significant part in this mechanism. The successful reform and modernization of the banking system will facilitate both integration with the world financial community and attraction of foreign capital to the country. Because of the deep crisis in production, it is foreign capital that is expected to give a serious initial impetus to the national economy.

■ VII. Mobilizing Household Savings

In the centrally planned economy, the financial structure and the financial instruments for mobilizing savings were poorly developed. Priority was given to centrally defined obligatory indicators based on product flows and connections. Monetary flows were of secondary importance. They were adapted to the requirements of the plan and the state budget.

The issue of the active role and influence of money, interest, credit, exchange rate, etc., did not exist at all. One example is the interest rate on demand deposits of the population with the SSB. When it was established in the 1950s, that rate was 4%. Later on it gradually decreased, reaching 1% in the 1980s. At the same time, there have been a number of price increases, although they were administratively ordered. Simultaneously, the amount of public savings grew considerably. Interest rates had little to do with the state of the economy and did not affect savings either. The public directed its savings to the SSB because it was the only institution to that end.

This situation was preserved until 1990, when savings began accumulating in commercial banks as well. A radical change in the field of savings could be observed with the launch of the economic reform in 1991. At its very beginning, when interest rates grew considerably, there was great interest in having deposits with the SSB and other banks, particularly in term deposits. For the first time, the real significance of interest rates could be felt. About one-third of the long-term housing credits of the public were redeemed in advance. Long queues of people lining up in front of the SSB and other banks to either transform old deposits or make new ones have been a particularly unpleasant and regrettable sight throughout the country since February 1991.

At present though, the banking system has few financial instruments to mobilize savings—only sight, time, and savings deposits, checking accounts, and some others are used. The need for diversifying the financial tools to attract the savings of the public is not widely recognized, however, because a considerable part of money savings and reserves were absorbed as a result of the large increase in prices. But when in the near future the national economy starts working and monetary flows normalize, this need will immediately emerge.

There are some concrete problems that banks are trying to solve by themselves or that will be solved in the course of the banking system restructuring: for instance, directing the public savings from the SSB to commercial banks and developing a bank subsidiaries network, the technical level of banking operations, and human relations in banks. So far it can be said that banks are trying to enhance their deposit operations mainly intuitively and sporadically, and not as a policy strategy. There is a lack of well-trained personnel who are familiar with and can implement more sophisticated tools for accumulating savings.

An important problem in this field is the underdevelopment of financial intermediation: there are almost no non-banking intermediaries. At the moment this is to the advantage of the SSB and the commercial banks. However, activities are being launched by other intermediaries, such as, for instance, insurance companies other than the State Insurance Institute. To the same end, pension funds and other specialized funds will be established and developed.

■ VIII. Banking Services to the Public and to Firms

Compared to the highly developed countries, the level of banking services in Bulgaria is very low. The term "banking services" refers to the banking institutions themselves and their operations, the technical equipment, and the competence and skills of bank staff. The replacement of the Western-style parliamentary state in 1944 with a totalitarian communist regime also meant the disappearance of the banking profession for a period of nearly half a century. Prewar Bulgaria had banks and bankers comparable to those in other European countries, but because of the "barter" nature of the planned economy, the profession was degraded. At the same time, the so-called revolution in banking and financing services developed in the rest of the world. The low level of banking services can be observed in all aspects. We can add only that the technical equipment is poor, in some places nonexistent, and operations are done manually. This slows down settlements and other operations and decreases efficiency.

Most banking operations are lacking in variety, due to the recent monopoly in banking, the lack of competition, the "barter" character of the economic links, and the predominance of state ownership with its prodigality. Evidence of the low level of banking services is the limited number of, for instance, crediting and intermediary banking operations. Present-day banks can hardly be called institutions that produce and offer varied, attractive financial products. A large number of bank managers and specialists are not aware of the significance of this fact. The problem will be further aggravated by enlarging foreign competition, for instance, in foreign exchange operations, for which there is almost no experience in most of the banks in Bulgaria.

These operations are rather new to a large number of the banks, which only started carrying them out in February 1991.

In the field of banking services the country also relies on foreign experience, which is already in use in various training courses and seminars with the participation of experts from abroad. By opening foreign bank subsidiaries, naturally there will be an import of know-how.

Until now there has been a certain division and differentiation between banking services for the public and for firms. With the reform of the banking system and the establishment of commercial banks, this differentiation will slowly disappear. It still exists, however, mainly because the SSB continues to monopolize operations with the public. There are no legal obstacles to such operations being performed in the other banks as well. This will be formalized by the Law on Banks and Crediting Activity, whose adoption by parliament is pending in the summer or autumn of 1991.

■ IX. The Central Bank's Role in Developing an Efficient Payments System

Under a centrally planned economy, there is in fact no central bank. The country had only one bank, the BNB, which through its branches and subsidiaries carried out all banking operations, including settlements. With such huge centralization of banking operations, administrative mechanisms played a crucial role in managing banking activities. Settlements were slow and inert and the forms of payment antiquated. But this was no hindrance for the system, because when there was a lack of money the payer automatically received a credit from the bank.

Presently the country is undergoing a transition to a two-tier banking system in which the central bank is the organizer and coordinator of the country's payment system. These obligations of the BNB stem from the new Law on the Central Bank, already in force. In mid-1991 the rules and regulations for performing payments were drafted and discussed; their adoption by the board of the BNB is pending. In general, these rules and regulations introduce European and world standards in the field of payments.

The establishment of a clearing system that will meet more modern requirements is being undertaken. An impediment is the poor level of technical equipment available in the banking system. Foreign experience will be studied and applied in this field.

■ X. Remaining Difficulties

In the restructuring of the banking system into a two-tier system, there are many difficulties and problems that have not yet been solved. There is, for instance, no system of insuring deposits. Bank supervision is neither sufficiently developed nor grounded on a modern foundation. A new law on accounting has recently been adopted, but applying European and world accounting standards is still slow. The automated processing of banking data is at a low level. As a whole, the banking system lacks sufficiently qualified and well-trained staff, people who are both enterprising and innovative. This is due to the fact that in the past the professional prestige of bank personnel was low. University education was not satisfactory. We should also take into account the psychological difficulties in adopting a modern banking system by people who are used to working in a passive environment, without ambitions, without real chances of professional promotion. The BNB is doing its best to be the initiator in training bank personnel. There is also bilateral cooperation, mostly with European countries, and in the autumn of 1991 a Banking Training Institute will be set up.

7

Banking Reform in Romania
EMIL IOTA GHIZARI

The fundamental restructuring of the banking system is an essential component of the transition process towards a market economy in Romania. Although it started only in early 1991, this process is already well outlined, and is reorienting the economy on a rational basis. It should be stressed from the very beginning that, in formulating the stages and the aims of the restructuring of the banking system, the Romanian authorities have extensively consulted with and followed the advice of experts at the IMF, the World Bank, and other international financial institutions, as well as experts at many European and non-European central banks. Cooperation in this respect provides very useful support for the National Bank of Romania.

■ I. General Framework of the Banking System Restructuring

The restructuring process includes two basic components: institutional and functional. The institutional component, which has largely been put in place, is aimed mainly at setting up a two-tier banking system. The upper tier is represented by the National Bank of Romania (NBR), which is to assume responsibility for all functions of a central bank: the formulation and conduct of monetary, credit, and exchange policy, and participation in foreign negotiations on financial, monetary, and payment issues. In addition, the NBR is the supervisory authority for all banking institutions. All these functions, fulfilled "de facto," are stipulated "de jure" in the

Emil Iota Ghizari is Deputy Governor of the National Bank of Romania.

Banking Act (Law No. 33/1991) and in the Status of the National Bank of Romania Act (Law No. 34/1991), which are already in force.

The second tier includes the commercial banks, set up as stock companies. Presently, the state-owned banking companies in operation are the Romanian Bank for Foreign Trade, the Romanian Bank for Development, Agrobank, the Savings Bank, and the Romanian Commercial Bank—an offspring of the National Bank of Romania in the banking system reorganization. After the state pays the subscribed capital fully, then the banks, which have complete functional autonomy, intend to improve their capitalization by floating shares. At the moment, the capital of these banks represents less than 4% of their assets, which is about half the level recommended by the Bank for International Settlements.

Three private banking companies are also operating in Romania, namely the Cooperative Bank "Bankcoop," the Bank for Small Industry and Free Enterprise "Mindbank," and the commercial bank "Ion Tiriac." Further, the institutional reorganization of the banking system also includes the establishment of banks specializing in import-export guarantee transactions and capital investment.

While paying attention to setting up new types of financial institutions, the National Bank is also concerned with the functional improvement of existing banks. In this process, the first step was to remove the monopoly of some state banks over specific economic branches. At present, any commercial company may keep an account with any bank, either private or state-owned, thus stimulating competition and increasing the quality of banking services. We are witnessing a higher volatility of deposits, with many companies transferring their accounts from one bank to another.

The second step is development of the interbank market; in this process the NBR's monopoly is being removed. The National Bank of Romania was, until now, the sole depository of the excess liquidity of the banks (presently, only the Savings Bank has excess liquidity) and also the sole refinancing source for all the banks. The direct transfer of the excess funds of the Savings Bank to other commercial banks is stimulated by the interest rate policy of the National Bank. In the future, a significant enlargement of interbank relations is expected, especially in short-term credit operations.

It is clear enough that there are major difficulties that must still be overcome. Some of the important tasks facing both the NBR and commercial banks include diversifying saving and credit instruments, introducing negotiable instruments, drawing up clear regulations concerning credit guarantees, and establishing a secondary market for securities. I think we can be optimistic: once this stiffly controlled market is deregulated and restructured, which is the task of the authorities, it will develop by itself.

■ II. Monetary Policy of the National Bank

The basic objective of monetary policy, clearly stated in the first article of the National Bank Statute, is the stability of the national currency. In 1991, however, price liberalization is expected to double the price level. In order to avoid price growth over this level, the National Bank has decided to curb the growth of the money supply, projecting a 15% rate for 1991. In order to accomplish this objective, the National Bank of Romania will use three main instruments in the first stage: interest rate controls, specific credit ceilings for banks, and refinancing policy. Reserve requirements will be subsequently introduced.

A. Interest Rate Policy

Interest plays virtually no role in the centrally planned economies. Interest rates applied in the Romanian economy were rather symbolic: 3%–5% on credits extended to economic units, and only 3% on refinancing credits granted by the National Bank. On January 1, 1991, in an attempt to turn the interest rate into an effective monetary tool, the NBR increased the general level of interest rates considerably: 7% for deposits of the Savings Bank with the National Bank, 8% for refinancing credits, and up to 11% for credits granted by the banks to economic institutions.

The new system has brought about two new developments: on the one hand, commercial banks negotiate the interest level with their clients, within the ceilings set by the NBR. On the other hand, as far as the interbank refinancing credits are concerned, an average interest rate of 8% was set, thus encouraging direct relationships among the commercial banks, without the intermediation of the National Bank.

It is encouraging that a money market has suddenly emerged after the announcement of the new interest rate policy. The volume of interbank transactions and transactions with other financial institutions—such as the insurance institutions—reached an amount of over 100 billion lei, which is more than 20% of the broad money supply. This was a first step only, a signal to economic institutions that the time of cheap money has passed. The next stage, starting April 1, 1991, was the full liberalization of interest rates, which now are determined on the basis of supply and demand.

Taking into account the high demand for liquidity and the ceilings set by the National Bank for growth of the money supply in the market, we can assume that interest rates will rise, reaching real positive levels by the action of market forces and not by administrative decisions of the NBR. In time this process will reduce the inflationary growth of the money supply and will lead to a better allocation of the financial and material resources in the economy.

B. Credit Ceilings

For the time being, the National Bank of Romania must continue to rely on direct methods of money control, including credit ceilings on individual banks, due to the lack of other appropriate monetary instruments and the institutional impediments already mentioned. The credit ceilings cannot be maintained over a sustained period, however, since their effectiveness erodes over time. The setting of quarterly credit ceilings is complicated by the instability of the bank's portfolio; it is also detrimental to competition among banks. As a result, the NBR is considering the possibility of adopting alternative approaches that would eliminate the disadvantages of the present pattern, without losing control of credit expansion. Such an approach would be to link the ceilings for each bank with its ability to attract deposits during the previous quarter.

C. Refinancing Policy

Currently, and for the foreseeable future, refinancing policy remains the main instrument on which the National Bank of Romania can rely for market-oriented monetary policy implementation. Therefore, a substantial improvement of refinancing policy has been a basic concern of the NBR's management. As a first step, starting on March 1, 1991, the mechanism by which branches of the National Bank refinance commercial banks through their branches will be abandoned, in favor of direct refinancing relationships between NBR headquarters and the headquarters of the commercial banks. For the time being, refinancing is ensured in the form of lines of credit, the size of which is proportional to the ceilings for each bank.

As a second stage, starting on April 1, 1991, short-term refinancing has been ensured by means of an auction mechanism. Consequently, the interbank interest rate will be deregulated, which will create incentives for real competition between banks. Obviously, the mechanism of setting credit ceilings will be adjusted accordingly. The adequate implementation of these monetary policy instruments cannot conceivably be other than interconnected. For example, a loosening in the system of credit ceilings for each bank could not be imagined without a certain interest level meant to stop the increase in liquidity demand. Also, an auction mechanism for short-term refinancing could not be operational without the relaxation of credit ceilings for each bank.

Simultaneously with monitoring the effects of these monetary policy measures, the National Bank of Romania, in cooperation with the commercial banks, will focus on the development of the money market and the introduction of new instruments, e.g., certificates of deposit and treasury bills. In the process of implementing a flexible, but firm, monetary policy, the NBR still faces many uncertainties. For example, we do not know for sure the reaction of economic institutions to the generalized liberalization of prices, interest rates, and foreign trade (implemented concomitantly with the opening of foreign exchange auctions). It is expected that the reaction will be positive: the economic decline will be stopped, growth will resume (even at a moderate rate), and a more efficient allocation of material and financial resources and more rational domestic relative prices will be achieved. This will be critical for avoiding a hyperinflationary spiral and subsequently for a relative relaxation of the restrictions on the growth of the money supply.

■ *III. Banking Supervision*

The rapid developments in the banking system and the evolving competitive environment necessitated the introduction of effective banking supervision. This has been assumed by the National Bank of Romania. The legal framework for prudential supervision is based on the new central banking and commercial banking legislation, which is aimed at protecting the interest of creditors and at maintaining the stability of the banking industry by preventing systemic risks. According to the commercial banking laws, all domestic banks and branch offices of foreign banks in Romania are subject to the supervision of the NBR. The Romanian system of prudential supervision allows for both on-site and off-site controls. The newly established Regulation and Supervision Department of the NBR is currently involved in drafting prudential regulations and is empowered to conduct regular surveillance of banks, relying on bank inspections and analyses of bank reports.

Banking companies are to be established as Romanian juridical persons in accordance with the provisions of the law that governs commercial companies; they cannot be established in the form of "companies with limited liability." The establishment, operation, and liquidation of branches of banks in Romania that are foreign juridical persons will be governed by the law concerning commercial companies, following the recognition of these banks as foreign juridical persons pursuant to the conditions established by Romanian law. The establishment in Romania of subsidiaries of a bank with foreign juridical personality will be done according to the provisions of the law concerning the operation in Romania of agencies of foreign companies and foreign economic organizations. A license from the NBR will be required to conduct banking business.

To enable Romanian banking supervisory authorities to analyze the soundness of banks on a regular basis, financial institutions must submit monthly returns and other requested information to the NBR. The leading banking company of a group is requested to present the monthly returns both for its own unit and for the group as a whole. The law on commercial banking states that banking companies are to employ certified accountants to audit and certify their balance sheets. Banking companies will publish their balance sheets accompanied by the certificate of the independent certified auditors as soon as they have been approved by their general meeting of shareholders or other competent authority pursuant to provisions of the law on commercial companies and to the provisions and rules issued by the NBR.

To protect the rights of depositors, the commercial banking law provides for establishing funds to insure deposits held by banking companies for the benefit of physical persons. These funds may be set up by public or private financial institutions or by the Romanian state. They will operate under a license issued by the NBR and under its supervision.

The prudential supervision of banks is in its infancy in Romania. Presently, the NBR Regulation and Supervision Department is involved in the development of a comprehensive off-site monitoring system based on a set of prudential regulations regarding capital adequacy, liquidity, loans to large customers, investment limits, etc. The NBR is assisted in this effort by a team of experts from the Netherlands Bank in the framework of IMF technical assistance. As regards on-site supervision, comprehensive and regular examinations of banks have not been yet developed, and the examination of assets quality remains to be done in Romania.

The implementation of prudential supervision has been complicated by structural factors, by many inadequacies in the banking sector's legal and administrative infrastructure. Laws on bankruptcy, treatment of collateral, and mortgages are still to be enacted. Next, accounting standards and a system of independent auditing must be set in place. Full implementation of the prudential rules before the recapitalization of banks is made difficult by the large share of nonperforming loans in the total assets of the Romanian banks. The problem of the "old" housing credit portfolio consisting of credits at low and fixed interest rates must also be solved.

The Romanian supervisory authorities are aware of the fact that the inadequate capitalization of banks and the related issues of bad loans are matters that should be addressed at the earliest possible time. This situation is to be improved by cleaning up bank portfolios and by injecting new capital. The government may replace the bank's bad loans with long-term bonds yielding a positive interest spread over the bank's cost of funds. The capital of the banks will grow over time, thanks to the elimination of problem loans and the positive net income flow from the government bonds, which will enable banks to issue new shares. This implies a close cooperation of the NBR with the Ministry of Finance and the banks involved.

■ *IV. Conclusion*

In summary, Romania has made great strides in reforming the system of money, banking, and credit. As in other centrally planned economies with a monobank system, a two-tier banking system was created. The legal and institutional mechanisms for the development of a commercial banking system are being developed. It is expected that a vibrant, market-oriented banking system will soon evolve.

8

Restructuring of the Monetary and Credit System of the USSR

VYACHESLAV S. ZAKHAROV

■ *I. Necessity for Restructuring*

Because of the economic and political changes taking place in the Soviet Union, the monetary and credit system must be reorganized. An important political change has been the more prominent role of the USSR Supreme Soviet as a legislative body. Our country's parliament has become more active in legislative processes, passing laws that were previously enacted by governmental decree. Considerable changes in politics have also arisen due to the declarations of sovereignty and economic independence of the member republics of the union.[1]

As for economics, it has become common knowledge that the country's economy must be transformed from a system of rigid centralized control to one of market relations. Also on the agenda are such goals as privatization of property, demonopolization of production, development of competitiveness, support of entrepreneurship, and land reform. Steps are being taken towards reforming the financial system, especially improving the system of money circulation and stabilizing the consumer market.

The banking system that existed until recently was adequate for the centralized system and satisfied the needs of the national economy. But the structure of banks and their types of

---

Vyacheslav S. Zakharov is Deputy Chairman of the Board of Gosbank.

1. The author and editors realize that much of the legal structure envisaged in this paper has been displaced by recent political events. However, the paper is valuable in that it provides an overview of political and economic thinking that is likely to prevail at the level of the republics. Further, if a unified currency and monetary union emerges, many of the principles outlined in the paper will resurface.—Eds.

activities formed under largely administrative control no longer meet modern requirements. The reorganization of the national credit system has become a part of the general "perestroika," focusing on credit relations and banking institutions. The transition from administrative to economic methods of management has triggered a desperate need for alterations in the activities of the banks.

The development of new types of business activity, including cooperative, individual, and profit-oriented activity, has increased demand for new banking services. The implementation of an active social policy required increased credit for consumer needs and more general banking services for the population. All these demands predetermine the role of banks in the reconstruction of the national economic system and the main trends of improvements in the banking system.

During the first stage of the credit reform in 1987–1988, the government-owned specialized banks, namely, Promstroibank, Agroprombank, and Zhilsotsbank, were established, and assumed commercial activities that were previously under the jurisdiction of the State Bank of the USSR (Gosbank). The status of Gosbank, the central bank of the USSR, was greatly modified. It has ceased operations with clients and has become a bank for the banks, retaining the functions of a note-issuing center.

The transition to a market economy demands radical changes in the monetary and credit spheres. It is necessary to completely utilize economic (as opposed to administrative) mechanisms to develop and introduce new methods of monetary control that are more appropriate for market relations.

The previous monetary and credit system was dominated by a conservative banking system, composed of national specialized banks, which did not allow real partnership with borrowers or free capital movements in the economy. Gosbank, until recently, did not possess any instruments of monetary control or efficient means for regulating credit. The interest rate policy was very inefficient: low interest rates created excessive credit demand, which made investments with very low profitability possible.

During the second stage of the banking reform, which began in August 1988, regional and sectoral commercial banks were actively established, on a joint-stock and shared basis, for universal and specialized fields of activities. The new banking institutions were organized as voluntary associations of government-owned enterprises, cooperatives and their unions, and social organizations. These voluntary associations aim at the accumulation and rational utilization of monetary resources in the development of a certain region, sector, subsector, or group of enterprises or cooperatives.

In the first two years of the second stage of the reform, the charters of more than 450 joint-stock commercial banks were registered. Among them were universal, cooperative, regional, sectoral, diversified, and innovation banks. The size of the banks varied greatly: their authorized capital share ranged from as low as 500,000 to as high as 300 million rubles.

Initially the banking system was modified according to instructions from above (the government). No modifications were made in response to initiatives from below. This point is important for understanding the new qualitative character of the current stage of reform, which reflects the development of initiative and entrepreneurship in the sphere of banking. New commercial banks contribute to the transformation to a market system by reducing monopoly and introducing competition in banking. Banking has become one of the main spheres of the economy in which real demonopolization is taking place. The newly established banks are noteworthy for their greater variety of banking activities, in that they are completely independent in their credit policy and not bound by centrally issued instructions in their day-to-day activities. The democratization of the banking system contributes to its efficiency and greatly decreases the danger that the system will be swallowed up by red tape. The banks' charters also provide for their rights to conduct business abroad.

The establishment of joint-stock commercial banks is the first step towards the creation of a money market. These banks independently determine their interest rates on loans and credits. Excess money balances now move not vertically but horizontally.

One should note, however, that the bulk of credit operations and banking services in the national economy were provided, until recently, by specialized government-owned banks, Promstroibank, Agroprombank, and Zhilsotsbank, which have more than 5,800 branches all over the country, much more than the total number of commercial banks. Under these conditions little competition between the joint-stock commercial banks and government-owned specialized banks can be expected.

The transition to a market economy requires an acceleration of the commercialization of banking. Thus the conversion of the specialized Agroprombank and Zhilsotsbank into joint-stock banks, which took place in the second half of 1990, was quite natural. Initially the action was supposed to take effect at the all-union level alone (as happened with Agroprombank), disregarding the fact that these banks serviced sectors subordinate to the local and republican authorities. However, the centrifugal trends present in our economy have led to the establishment of joint-stock banks on republican, regional, and district levels. It is possible that continued development of the economy will induce small banks to merge and establish larger banks and banking associations, but these actions will be at the intiative of the banks themselves. At this point the banks are more bent on individualization rather than the creation of associations. As of mid-February 1990, the USSR banking system consisted of:

1. Gosbank, the central bank of the USSR.
2. The central banks of the Russian Federation, Lithuania, Latvia, and Estonia. Central banks in other republics are in the process of being established.
3. Commercial banks:
   - all-union level: Vneshekonombank, Promstroibank, Agroprombank, and Sberbank (Savings) with their branches;
   - more than 1,380 regional and sector-oriented commercial and cooperative banks (the process of setting up joint-stock banks is still going on, so the total is likely to change).

■ *II. Basic Principles of Operation of the Banking System of the USSR in 1991*

The State Bank of the USSR and the republican central banks together form the system of central banks, which is based on a unified currency and is designed to function as a reserve system. Its functions include:

- issuing money and organizing its circulation;
- acting as lenders of last resort to commercial banks;
- organizing interbank payments;
- servicing the national debts of the USSR and of the republics;
- conducting open market operations, buying and selling foreign exchange on the free market;

- issuing licenses to commercial banks for conducting banking operations, including those connected with foreign exchange;
- supervising the activities of commercial banks.

In providing these functions, the State Bank of the USSR and the republican central banks as a unified system have the following basic aims:
- maintaining the stability of the unified currency;
- conducting unified national credit, monetary, and foreign exchange policies;
- protecting the interests of creditors and depositors of the banks, by defining uniform rules (for all participating republics) that regulate the activities of commercial banks, and by strictly supervising their adherence;
- assisting economic development and the creation of a unified market of the USSR and its integration into the world market.

The activities of Gosbank in 1991 are regulated by the Law on the State Bank of the USSR, according to which Gosbank is subordinate to the Supreme Soviet of the USSR and independent of executive bodies. Gosbank has the exclusive right to issue money in the form of bank notes and coins, which are unconditionally guaranteed by Gosbank's assets. Gosbank determines the types of payment documents (denominated in rubles) to be circulated on USSR territory. Gosbank regulates the ruble's exchange rate by establishing official rates and conducting operations of buying and selling foreign exchange for rubles on the free foreign exchange market. The use of foreign exchange and securities on the territory of the USSR is allowed only after obtaining permission from the State Bank of the USSR, which determines the procedure and the sphere of their circulation. Gosbank manages the gold and foreign exchange reserves that are on its balance sheet and act as a guarantor of its liabilities. For that purpose, the Ministry of Finance of the USSR transmits to Gosbank national gold reserves, which are adequate for establishing the national monetary stabilization fund.[2]

Operations involving custody and placement of these reserves are conducted by Gosbank independently or through authorized banks and institutions. A decision has been made

---

2. Many of these functions may be transferred to the republics or new nation states created from these republics if they become independent.

that the foreign exchange reserves will be deposited on international markets by Vneshekonombank by order of the State Bank of the USSR and on behalf of Vneshekonombank. Gosbank continues to represent the country's interests in relations with foreign central banks, international banks, and other financial and credit institutions. Currently, the republican central banks' activities associated with the functioning of the reserve system are regulated by the Law on the State Bank of the USSR, and those activities outside the framework of the reserve system, by republican banking laws.

The highest managing body of the central banks' system regarding the implementation of the functions of the reserve system is the Central Council of the State Bank of the USSR, which includes the chairman of Gosbank, the chairman's first deputy, and ten members, including the chairs of the republican central banks or other authorized representatives of the republics. The economic independence of republics still requires their obligatory participation in the process of designing monetary and credit policy.

The Central Council makes decisions on all principal problems of the functioning of the unified system of central banks, namely:

- it adopts the draft of the Main Guidelines on National Monetary and Credit Policy;
- it defines the volume and types of operations of Gosbank and the republican central banks on the bond market and on the free foreign exchange market with commercial banks, the all-union and republican budgets;
- it sets the interest rates on the operations of Gosbank and republican central banks with commercial banks, and with the all-union and republican budgets;
- it approves the limits of obligatory reserves of the commercial banks to be deposited with Gosbank and republican central banks, and other economic regulations encompassing banking activities.

The Central Council decisions are adopted, as a rule, by a simple majority vote of its members present at the meeting. Adoption of decisions on specific issues calls for a two-thirds majority. The execution of the Central Council's decisions are obligatory for all banks in the union.

Commercial banks provide services to legal bodies or private individuals under agreements or contracts. They may differ according to the following factors:

- the types of ownership of the authorized capital and the method of its establishment, e.g., joint-stock companies, associations with limited responsibility, associations with foreign capital participation, foreign banks, or others;
- the range of operations—universal or specialized;
- the territory of activities—national, republican, or regional;
- the sectoral orientation.

Banks may be established by legal bodies and private individuals, except members of Councils of People's Deputies at all levels (including their executive bodies, political organizations, and specialized and social funds). The share of participation of any founder or stockholder (participant) should not exceed 35% of the total volume of authorized capital. Special commercial banks may be established to finance national, republican, and other projects, according to procedures developed by the national and republican legislatures. All commercial banks are independent of executive and governmental bodies in making decisions pertaining to regular banking activities. Government officials are not allowed to participate in the bank's managing bodies, even on a part-time basis.

A commercial bank operates on the basis of licenses for banking operations (special licenses are needed for dealing in foreign exchange) issued by its republican central bank. As regards all-union commercial banks, Gosbank is responsible for issuing licenses. In cases determined by law, Gosbank or a republican central bank can decline an application for a license or withdraw one that has already been issued. Commercial banks or their founders may appeal decisions taken by Gosbank or the republican central bank to the courts while continuing operations.

Commercial banks may open their branches and representative offices in the USSR and abroad according to the established procedure. But they are independent in setting up interest rates and commissions on their operations. All commercial banks are endowed with the right to attract deposits on their own conditions. Upon receipt a bank must provide for the money's safekeeping and duly fulfill the bank's obligations to depositors. To attain this aim, commercial banks must start interbank deposit insurance funds according to the procedures and set conditions determined by the corresponding republican central bank.

In order to coordinate their activities and protect their interests, commercial banks may establish unions, associations, and other institutions. The latter must not be used to engage in activities directed at monopolization of the banking market, such as formulating interest rates, setting up commissions, or limiting competition in banking.

The State Bank of the USSR sets up regulations in the following areas for commercial banks:

- minimum volume of authorized capital;
- ratio between bank's own capital and its assets;
- indicators of liquidity;
- volume of obligatory reserves to be deposited with Gosbank and the republican central banks;
- maximum risk for a single borrower;
- maximum foreign exchange, interest, and exchange rate risks.

Gosbank is also to adopt rules of bookkeeping in commercial banks concerning the substance and volume of bank reports and other documents provided by the latter for Gosbank and republican central banks. Commercial banks publish their annual balance sheets and balance of their profits and losses after authentication by an authorized auditor. It is necessary to establish a wide network of auditor companies with trained staff, and until the creation of such a network, the task will be done by the inspection and audit services of the republican central banks or Gosbank.

There are considerable peculiarities in the functioning of Vneshekonombank, Promstroibank, and Sberbank. Vneshekonombank has been withdrawn from the control of the Foreign Economic Commission of the Council of Ministers of the USSR, though it retains its original functions. The bank will gradually be transformed into a joint-stock commercial bank, shaping its status in accordance with the provisions of its credit agreements with foreign countries. The all-union and republican governments have taken measures to completely repay foreign loans obtained by Vneshekonombank according to the decisions made by the Council of Ministers of the USSR and losses incurred by credits given by the bank to foreign and national institutions under the government's instructions. Vneshekonombank retains the status of authorized agent of the government in terms of borrowing money abroad, servicing the debt, and deploying national foreign exchange resources.

Promstroibank is the official government agent for financing large-scale all-union projects with support from the budget. At the end of 1991 steps are to be taken to transform it into a joint-stock commercial bank.

Sberbank is retained as a USSR national property; it is a specialized commercial bank that conducts operations to attract and utilize household savings. The safekeeping and repayment of deposits is guaranteed by Gosbank. The money is utilized by Sberbank for credits to private individuals and for other purposes, including the deployment of governmental securities of the USSR and of the republics. The transfer of branches of Sberbank to the republics and the establishment of republican savings banks independently of the USSR may take place since republics must finance a proportional part of the state debt from their territory's savings.

■ *III. Monetary and Credit Regulation*

The changes that have taken place recently in monetary and credit regulation touched upon four factors:

- The subjects of monetary and credit relations. Instead of several super-large state-owned banks, many joint-stock banks appeared.
- The objects of the regulation. Previously, Gosbank separately regulated cash and non-cash circulation: now the object of control is the entire money supply.
- Methods of regulation of money and credit relations. Instead of credit and cash plans per se, Gosbank employs internationally approved economic methods of money supply regulation.
- Mechanisms for making decisions. Previously the decisions were made by the government and by the Board of Governors of the State Bank of the USSR. Now they are made by the Supreme Soviet and by the Central Council of Gosbank, including representatives of the republics.

The country's money supply is regulated by Gosbank and republican central banks on the basis of the Main Guidelines on National Monetary and Credit Policy, which are approved annually by the Supreme Soviet at the same time as the national plan and the budget. The Main Guidelines include:

- analysis and forecast of economic cycles, coupled with indicators of social and economic development performance of the union and of the republics, and the union and republican budgets;

- economically justified limits of the money supply;
- targets for foreign exchange and interest policies;
- the main methods of monetary and credit regulation.

The term "money supply" is defined here as the amount of cash, money in accounts and deposits of legal bodies and private individuals, and other unconditional monetary liabilities of the banks. For that purpose, aggregate M2, which includes cash money, all money in accounts, and money in short-term deposits, is employed. With more experience, the methods of calculation and regulation of the money supply will be improved.

The main economic methods of money supply regulation are currently:

- determination of the volume of credits provided by Gosbank and republican central banks to commercial banks;
- operations with securities and foreign exchange;
- determination of obligatory reserve requirements deposited by commercial banks with Gosbank and republican central banks;
- interest rate policy.

Due to the ineffectiveness of the money and credit markets, commercial banks are forced to apply mostly to Gosbank for credits. Gosbank credits make up almost three-fourths of all interbank credits, making its role in regulating credit relations relatively large. This influence will diminish with the development of money and credit markets. Besides Gosbank, the republican central banks and Sberbank are also becoming lenders. Until recently the Savings Bank had to deposit its resources with Gosbank, utilizing only 3% for lending to the population. In 1991 the Savings Bank was granted the right to use the accumulation of deposits independently, making it a significant participant in the money and credit markets.

Until recently, Gosbank used its "centralized" resources in state-owned specialized banks according to credit plans made annually. In 1991 this procedure will be retained with regard only to commercial banks having all-union importance: Promstroibank and Agroprombank. For the former Zhilsotsbank (housing), which has lost its all-union structure, and the commercial banks (including those established on the basis of former specialized banks), the deployment of centralized resources will be distributed by republican central banks or directly by Gosbank.

The state-owned specialized banks previously received their resources under a plan from a special fund and could freely deploy them. Now they have to attract their resources from the market, an activity to which they are not accustomed. Taking this into account, the need to establish special broker companies and to employ other forms of attracting credit resources becomes evident.

The extent of Gosbank's influence on the money supply depends on the current state of the national budget and options for financing the deficit. In 1986–1990 the credit investments of banks in the national economy suffered a 30% decline (an absolute decline of 157 billion rubles). This, however, did not cause a reduction in the money supply, as the whole increase in the credit fund for the five years and the credit reduction were redirected to financing the budget deficit. The allocation of an enormous sum of credit resources to the budget deficit then requires an accelerated issue of money to cover regular credit demands of the economy.

Before 1990 the national budget deficit was directly covered by the borrowing of the Ministry of Finance of the USSR from Gosbank. Having issued 74 billion rubles' worth of governmental securities in 1990, the Ministry of Finance has sold only 59.8 billion rubles, out of which 49.1 billion rubles' worth, or 82%, were bought by Gosbank. Various enterprises and cooperatives subscribed for only 17.5 million rubles' worth of these securities, and commercial banks only 11.6 million. The population bought more than 4 billion rubles' worth of securities, which were mostly special certificates for durable goods.

In many countries, central banks are the main holders of government debt, but that does not mean that they have to finance budget deficits directly, or ineffectively utilize their credit resources for the same purpose. It is essential to make government-issued bonds more attractive to enterprises and private individuals. Then the bonds will be willingly bought by the banks with the possibility of their subsequent resale in the secondary market. Only if a secondary market develops will Gosbank's operations on the open market be effective in keeping the money supply at a certain level.

The fact that one part of the government debt (pre-1990) is interest-free, while another bears no maturity dates, cannot, however, be considered normal. Under these conditions the budget presupposes practically no resources for financing the government debt. The 1991 budget allocates only about 12 billion rubles for the purpose of debt financing, while the government debt stands at 540 billion rubles. The Ministry of Finance is trying to avoid servicing the government debt. This avoidance artificially undervalues the budget deficit. The Supreme Soviet of the USSR has passed a resolution charging the government to take steps to settle the debt of the Ministry of Finance to Gosbank by 1991.

Gosbank may also influence the money supply by buying or selling foreign exchange for rubles. Gosbank has been assigned the authority to set up the procedures and range of operations with foreign currencies, and payment documents (checks, drafts, bonds) in rubles and foreign exchange. In the present environment, foreign exchange/rubles intervention is obviously required. However, this measure will hardly be effective under the conditions of parallel circulation of foreign exchange in the economy.

Minimum reserve requirements, initially 5% of the deposited funds, were established for commercial banks by Gosbank in 1989, and for state-owned specialized banks in 1990. Later the rate was increased to 10% and in 1991 a further increase is planned. At the same time the intent is to base reserve requirements on the quality of banks' liabilities, mostly regarding maturities.

Commercial banks' interest rate policy towards companies is of great importance. Until recently the average interest rate on state-owned bank loans was about 2.5%. Such a low rate had historical causes and did not correspond to the real value of money. Joint-stock commercial banks charge rates several times higher, but they have only a small share of loans extended.

In order to limit the demand for loans and, hence, squeeze the money supply, new higher interest rates, mandatory for all banks, were introduced for the period of November 1, 1990 to May 1, 1991:

- for loans of up to one year—6% per annum;
- from one to three years—up to 9% per annum;
- over five years—up to 11% per annum.

On arrears, high-risk loans, or loans unsecured by pledge, guarantees, or covenant, a rate of up to 25% per annum may be charged. In certain cases lower interest rates might have been preserved, provided that they are enumerated at the expense of bodies that have authorized such subsidized loans.

In the future, interest rates, together with price liberalization in industry and trade, will move to their real level. However, there are proposals to protect against adverse movements of the economy, preserving control of interest rates on active operations of commercial banks until the end of 1991. Simultaneously the regulating role of Gosbank will also be extended. It will exercise its role through the establishment of interest rates on loans extended to commercial banks. This rate has been set at 8% per annum for the first quarter of 1991; later it will be increased.

The efficacy of interest rate policies depends on the established procedure of allocating interest costs at the enterprise level. The Law on Taxation on Enterprises, Concerns and Organizations provides for ascribing interest costs on short-term loans, with minor exceptions, to manufacturing costs (workmanship, services). Only interest on long-term loans are paid out of profits. Previously, all interest payments have been paid out of profits.

The abovementioned policy of allocating interest costs was designed to squeeze the demand for industrial loans from enterprises operating on wholesale as well as procurement prices fixed by the government. Any deliberate increase in manufacturing costs by the producer (with the ultimate intent of raising their own wholesale prices), in particular via payment of higher interest on credit, will bite into their profits. Later, when the majority of prices are contracted between manufacturers and consumers, the policy of allocating interest costs to manufacturing costs will eliminate the economic effect. Some enterprises, especially monopolists, will assent to paying high rates of interest, given the legal authority to attribute interest charges to manufacturing costs, and hence to producer prices. However, not a single buyer or price-controlling authority will be able to dispute such a practice. Buyers will also have to bear the burden of commercial banks' interest costs of refinancing facilities provided by Gosbank. As production demonopolization and deficit liquidation continue, enterprises will be interested in reducing their production costs, thus, the interest rate policy will become more efficient. It is difficult to expect this scenario or a decrease in the demand for loans in the nearest future, however.

In order to pursue an effective monetary and credit policy and enable commercial banks to function more successfully, banking credit portfolios were cleared. More than 100 billion rubles' worth of credits that had been extended previously and had poor repayment prospects were written off from the balance sheets of the agricultural enterprises and some other sectors at the expense of the all-union and republican governments.

The transition to a market economy is greatly hampered by the excessive purchasing power of enterprises and the population and the widening imbalance between goods and money on the wholesale and consumer markets. Under these conditions it is necessary to attract the excess money into long-term deposits and into enterprise accounts. The main goals are to increase interest rates to compensate for money devaluation and to develop new types of personal savings. A decision has been taken to increase interest rates on personal accounts in the Savings Bank. Until recently the rate was 3% per annum on deposits of over one year. As of November 1, 1990, the rate was 5% per annum for deposits of one to three years, 7% per annum for more than three and up to seven years and 9% for more than five years. This measure should stabilize deposits; the share of long-term accounts will increase. People who had savings in cash became interested in depositing them with a bank.

The rates for deposits of enterprises, organizations, and cooperatives varied within 2%–8% per annum, depending on the duration. Of course, these rates as well as interest on saving accounts can only partly compensate for inflation.

The increase of interest rates on household savings and enterprise deposits strengthened the role of the banking system in attracting household savings for crediting preferential programs. For example, the money of small depositors is directed by banks towards financing the privatization of property.

In the case of unstable overshooting of the money supply targets and price increases, if the abovementioned methods are ineffective in countering the inflation, other additional steps might be taken. These include limiting the loan facilities of commercial banks and imposing ceilings on interest rates of both assets and liabilities as well as on commissions charged. These measures would be temporary and employed selectively, depending on the type of bank, the kind of credit, the sector, and the geographical location. Taking into consideration the national foreign debt management policy, Gosbank may limit the amount of foreign loans to commercial banks.

■ IV. Commercial Bank Supervision and Auditor Organizations

According to the bank legislation, Gosbank determines certain indicators (for commercial banks) directed at protecting the interests of lenders and clients. The new banks should function in tougher conditions right from the start. Their stability will depend on it. The banks should be tougher with their clients, who will face hard loans at last. The image of a bank as an organization that has to help everyone, everywhere, is disappearing. There are other options however, to encourage development of private initiative (e.g., softening up requirements for operation of commercial banks for the time being).

In commercial bank supervision, the following economic and balance liquidity indicators are currently used:

1. Bank's own capital-liabilities ratio:
   $K1 = C/L$, where
   C = bank's own capital;
   L = bank's liabilities.

The K1 figures should not run lower than 1/12 for major commercial banks and 1/20 for other commercial banks. Most banks have not attained the maximums allowed according to the overall performance of commercial banks. As of June 1, 1991, the ratio was 1/8.

2. Personal savings bank's own capital ratio:
   $K2 = S/C$, where
   S = personal savings (deposit liabilities);
   C = bank's own capital.

The K2 figures should not exceed 1.0. This factor is looked upon as temporary, necessary until the personal accounts in the commercial banks' insurance system become active. So far these banks have not shown interest in attracting personal savings, probably because of labor costs involved and technical deficiencies. As of June 1, 1991, only 503 million rubles were attracted under the program, the figure being dozens of times lower than the banks' own capital.

3. Maximum risk indicator for single borrower:
   $K3 = K/C$, where
   K = total indebtedness on loans to a single borrower plus 50% of over-balance liabilities regarding the borrower;
   C = bank's own capital.

The K3 figure should not exceed 0.5. If loans are extended to the shareholders of the bank, or to those connected with the bank on the managerial level, the amount of loans to a single borrower should not exceed 30% of the bank's own capital.

Where K3 exceeds 15% of the bank's own capital, the loan is considered "large." "Large" loans are subject to special supervision of the bank's management and may be proffered only in cases of a full "pro" vote of the commercial bank's council. The total sum of "large" loans given by the bank as of the end of the month must not exceed more than eight times the total of the bank's own capital. The total amount of the five biggest "large" loans (considering the over-balance liabilities too) should not exceed more than three times the bank's own capital. All information on "large" loans must be submitted on the first day of each month. Single loans of one million rubles or more should be immediately reported by the commercial bank or the branch in question to the local Gosbank office.

4. Current Liquidity Indicator:
   $K4 = Q/Lc$, where
   Q = bank's liquid assets, including loans and other types of payments in the bank's favor with a one-month maturity;
   Lc = bank's liabilities on call accounts, including deposits, loans taken, and guarantees extended by the bank with a one-month maturity.

The K4 figure should not be lower that 0.3. For commercial banks not dealing with cash payments services, the K4 figure should not be less than 0.5.

5. Long-Term Liquidity Indicator:
   $K5 = M/(C+Ld)$, where
   M = loans extended by the bank with at least three years to maturity;
   C = bank's own capital;
   Ld = bank's liabilities on deposit accounts and loans, taken by the bank with maturity over three years.

K5 should not exceed 1.0.

Republican central bank or Gosbank local offices are to supervise the implementation of these regulations in commercial banks. Supervision is based on the bank's monthly reports (should branches and representative offices exist—on consolidated balance reports), with special annexes on K1, K2, K3, K4, and K5 indicators. Ten days after the date of analysis, a short statement is issued, to be examined by the head of the local

Gosbank office. Gosbank officers should also ensure that the authorized capital of a commercial bank is paid from sources and within periods stated in the bank's statutory documents.

In case of violations of the set indicators, Gosbank offices are to send a written order to the commercial bank to take steps towards improving its financial condition, and bringing the liquidity indicators in line with those assigned, within one month's time. To monitor the implementation of the above measures, Gosbank offices may demand the submittal of reports showing evidence that the necessary measures have been taken.

If the commercial bank violates the regulations, fails to follow Gosbank's and/or the republican central bank's instructions, submits false reports, or pursues unprofitable operations on a regular basis, or if a situation endangering the interests of investors and lenders arises, Gosbank or the republican central bank may initiate alternative sanctions. For example, it may address the bank's founders with the demand for an increase of the bank's own capital, a restructuring of the bank's assets, or a reorganization or liquidation of the bank.

If these orders are not fulfilled, the following sanctions may be incurred:

- penalties charged on the amount of additional profit received by the bank through misoperation;
- compulsory increase of minimum reserves;
- assignment of a temporary administration to manage the bank during the rehabilitation period;
- withdrawal of the license for banking activities.

During the first two and a half years of reform, four commercial banks had their licenses withdrawn, while two others were subjected to other sanctions.

Gosbank's supervisory efficiency greatly depends on the truthfulness of the data it is given. Thus, the creation of independent auditor companies, called upon to check the commercial bank's reports and the legitimacy of their operations, is becoming ever more important. The existence of external auditors will also contribute to a better basis for bank and client relations, making the clients feel more secure.

Due to the sophistication of the banking system under reform, the rapid growth of the number of commercial banks and the diversification of their operations, the bank supervision system must be constantly improved. Effective supervision is one of the prerequisites put forward by foreign banks before they become involved, so as to be sure that their interests are protected. Overall, the involvement will call for the cooperation of Soviet auditors with their foreign counterparts.

The solution to the problem is greatly facilitated by the participation of Soviet delegations in regular international conferences on bank supervision. At the last conference, held in October 1990 in Frankfurt, Germany, a decision was made to form a regional group of experts from the Soviet Union and the countries of Eastern Europe to trade their experience, since they have similar problems in developing a banking system during the transition to a market economy. In March 1991 the first meeting of the regional group was held in Budapest. It was decided to hold such meetings on a regular basis, once or twice a year in different countries.

V. Further Development of the Monetary and Credit Systems

The efficiency of Gosbank's influence on the money supply is decreasing, because the formation of market structures in our national economy is generally lagging behind banking reforms. Privatization of property, demonopolization of production, liberalization of prices, and other measures are long overdue. There is now an acute danger that banks will break off from the other institutions, while they are needed to preserve the status quo. Thus, the task is to direct the activities of the banks by economic methods in order to solve current problems of the economy, without hampering their further commercialization.

Banking activities are considerably curbed by the lack of scientifically substantiated and well-tested economic development criteria, such as accurate price indices and unemployment measures. This greatly impedes the adoption of Gosbank's decisions on the regulation of the money supply. We are groping our way in the dark, through a method of trial and error, which might make the situation in our economy even worse.

The economy cannot be stabilized until the purchasing power of the ruble is restored. Foreign and national history shows that all good intentions to stabilize the domestic economy are doomed to failure unless they are based on hard money. The weak ruble has no respect anywhere. Everyone is trying to get rid of money, to invest it in goods or valuables. Moreover, the goods for money cycle is being replaced by goods for goods trade. The introduction of food and consumer goods coupons, and the parallel (sometimes preferential) circulation of foreign exchange are bringing about a further devaluation of the national currency. Soviet money is ceasing to be a general equivalent and a legal means of payment.

It is difficult to believe that the dollar or some other foreign exchange will replace the ruble for internal circulation. Steps should be taken to strengthen the ruble instead of weakening it. The instability of our national currency is an obstacle that we will always face while solving economic (and other) problems. Is it necessary to solve the problem of stabilizing the monetary system first and only then start tackling other goals? It is not that simple: one should not isolate or underestimate the problem of ruble devaluation: its solution is the link that we can use to pull ourselves out of our other problems.

This also determines the role of the banking system in economic stabilization. We had long-lasting illusions that the activity of a bank, with the help of money circulation, reflects the real processes in the economy. Therefore a bank always played a secondary role as a guide and accountant of money circulation. Of course all banks play this role. Mediation in payments is one of the first and foremost functions of a bank. Before payment, however, one has to have something to pay with. The fact that banks "produce" money as a specific good was generally known, but special attention was paid to cash circulation. Meanwhile there was a tendency to ignore the fact that for the most part a bank "produces" only money entries in its books (about 9/10 of the total), and that there are economic laws regulating the total money supply and not only its cash part.

It is time for us to admit that the banking system must play an independent role. The rule suggesting that "the one who spends must not issue" has to be accepted. Not long ago the Law on the State Bank of the USSR withdrew Gosbank from central government control. The problem is in freeing up the bank from its present guidance. If Gosbank's supervisor is replaced, that is not enough.

In its activities Gosbank must follow objective economic laws and those legal instructions that do not contradict economic ones. Accepting great independence, Gosbank accepts great responsibilities as well. The high professionalism of banking experts means not only utilization of their own knowledge and experience, but close cooperation with the competent bodies, taking into account the interests of all parts involved with money circulation.

The granting of the right to license banking operations to republican central banks must not lead to a decrease of control or the introduction of numerous loopholes to bypass existing regulations. This type of adverse activity would produce many improper competitors, (i.e., banks operating under different conditions). This is not to say, however, that the republics with the weakest regulations will be those with the most banks. "Competition" in this field will cause growing instability of banks. Their bankruptcies will cause corresponding effects on the economy. The next reasonable alternative to this "competition" is the creation and functioning of a system of general nationwide banking regulations. The regulations should be worked out with direct participation of the republican central banks. The commercial banks' supervising conditions also must be the same everywhere. Even now many commercial banks have set up their branches in the republics, and the process will probably continue.

Concentration of shares in the hands of a few founders is also creating conflicts of interests. Sometimes the founders obtain preferential credits at the expense of the bank itself or some other borrowers. In this respect one of the aims of Gosbank and the emerging auditor firms is to make the commercial banks follow strict norms for crediting shareholders. Also, as mentioned above, local authorities cannot be the founders of commercial banks. This does not seem to be a vital limitation and one can hope it will be changed in the future so that local authorities will be able to establish municipal banks.

Overall, the commercialization of banking will put forward the question of credit support for a few sectors of the national economy with regular loan coverage for the bulk of goods supply; cooperatives—85–90%, supply-sale organizations—65–70%, government (state) trade—50%. Many commercial banks will not risk providing loans to cover all the abovementioned goods. To increase their creditworthiness, these organizations must take immediate steps to increase their turnover funds, by decreasing their economic motivation (stimulation) funds.

One should expect changes in investment policies to develop simultaneously with changes in commercial policies. For instance, existing commercial banks are not willing to finance the existing extra long-term construction projects. At least, prior to providing loans, they will run a thorough check on the project, including its creditworthiness and availability of all necessary supplies and equipment to finish the job. The interest rates will inevitably increase as the loan repayment period becomes longer. This situation will lead to more responsibility on the part of the clients, making them apply for credits only in exceptional cases, with short maturity terms where payments can be returned before the project's end. Prior to complete commercialization in banking, we have to decide now on the future of extra long-term construction projects (e.g., find other sources of financing, feasibility of withdrawing them from use or sell-off of unfinished installations, etc.)

Commercial banks' own capital tends to grow with ongoing commercialization. As of January 1, 1988 the sum was 5.4 billion rubles. By January 1, 1991 the sum was close to 25 billion rubles. In three years, enterprises and cooperatives have invested about 20 billion rubles in commercial banks' stocks, thereby reducing their purchasing power by the same amount. Of course, these funds are now directed at the financing requirements of the enterprises, but on a higher rate of return basis. Therefore, the establishment of commercial banks favors the improvement of the real-to-financial equilibrium of the economy.

The increase in the share of the banks' own resources in their total pool of credit investments increases the stability of the banking system. The important factor is that these funds can be used to cover losses, which tend to increase in market environments. Investments in the equity of commercial banks are a source of extra profits for bank founders and shareholders. To maximize their profits, banks should candidly consider every loan agreement, favoring highly profitable and more competitive borrowers. Enjoying the return on equity, bank shareholders, however, will not accept offering subsidized loans.

No less important for the banking system is the goal of intermediation in settlements. The importance of this aim drastically increases in the market economy. One of the aims of Gosbank is the creation of an effective payment mechanism. At the end of 1991 the existing payment system will be replaced by a new system based on correspondent relations. The introduction of the network of Gosbank's clearing centers for operating the correspondent accounts of commercial banks does not exclude the introduction of local clearing systems between affiliates of large banks or directly between banks.

It should be mentioned that the problems of overdue payments lie largely with the payers themselves, who should transfer sufficient funds to honor all their outstanding obligations. The era when banks cushioned this mechanism by regular injections of loan payments is gone. Many enterprises presently cannot do without such cushioning, causing delays in payments. During the last months the mutual indebtedness of enterprises has grown considerably and has reached 61 billion rubles. This greatly complicates the situation of suppliers who have to push the demand for loans to make up for the inadequacy of payment receipts.

Factoring operations, which are new for our banks, soften the payment problems; their total as of June 1, 1991 amounts to 6.3 billion rubles. There is potential for the granting of legal status for commercial credit operations and the establishment of commercial bills circulation.

Non-cash payments of the population can also be referred to as a less developed banking operation. Nowadays only Sberbank carries out such operations. The development of a regime for non-cash payments of the population is hampered by the lack of the necessary equipment and long-distance communications facilities.

A very acute problem is the attraction of foreign capital for the development of banking activities. By the middle of 1991, 73 representative offices of foreign banks were accredited with the State Bank of the USSR, but there were no branches that could carry out banking operations. At the end of 1989, International Moscow Bank, the first joint-venture bank, was established. The Soviet founders and shareholders of the bank are Vneshekonombank, Promstroibank, and Sberbank. Foreign partners include Banca Commerciale Italiana (Italy), Bayerische Landesbank (Germany), Creditanstalt-Bankverein (Austria), Credit Lyonnais (France), and Kansallis Osake Pankki (Finland). The registered authorized capital of the bank is 100 million rubles. Soviet partners have shares not exceeding 40 million rubles, half of which is in hard currencies. All foreign partners have equal shares of capital.

Soviet banks are not active in the creation of a network abroad. Vneshekonombank has a branch in Zurich and representative offices in 10 countries: Algeria, Argentina, the Czech and

Slovak Federal Republic, China, Egypt, Hungary, India, Italy, Syria, and Turkey. There is also an intention to establish foreign branches of Vneshekonombank and other commercial banks that have obtained general licenses for foreign economic operations.

To broaden and facilitate credit services for entrepreneurship, farming, and leasing activities, it will be useful to rehabilitate the credit cooperatives that existed before 1930 as independent forms of cooperative activities (along with manufacturing and consumer cooperatives). It is the credit cooperative sector that still exists and successfully operates in many countries at different stages of development. Leaseholders, farmers, and those living in rural and suburban areas involved in individual labor activity can unify in credit cooperatives. The establishment of a wide network of such cooperatives throughout the country will bring them closer to individual customers and help solve a number of problems. First, they might help to accumulate personal savings now kept in mattresses, socks, etc. Second, they could facilitate the procurement of loans for members for the development of economic activity. Finally, the establishment of credit cooperatives will contribute to the further democratization of banking activity and involve the broader public in business. Aware of the living standards of their members, cooperatives will establish their credit and interest rate policies accordingly. They should have the right to participate in the establishment of cooperative banks and take out loans in other banks of their choice.

There are some unsolved taxation problems for commercial banks in the present legislation. Payments to the state budget are fixed at 60% of commercial banks' balance sheet profits. Certain redemptions to insurance and banking technology development funds, up to 20% of gross profits, but not more than that actually allocated for those purposes are tax-free prior to payments to the state. After-tax profits are reallocated for expansion of the banking business, including the increase of authorized capital, corporate investments, payment of dividends, bonuses for employees, training of personnel, and advertising and presentation activities. There are views that part of the expenditures should be covered by pre-tax profits or ascribed to operational costs. Banks should probably have some tax subsidies, depending on the type of business done and the character of operations performed.

As this section details, the problems of further development of the money and credit systems are many. Day by day these problems are being addressed. Rapid political change further complicates the creation of a unified monetary system. Nonetheless, these issues lie at the heart of the transition and must be solved either at the union or republic level.

9

Financial Reform in Eastern Europe and the USSR

TADAIE YAMASHITA

■ *I. Introduction*

From the previous papers, it is quite evident that countries in transition have courageously initiated a comprehensive reform of their respective financial systems, and that, in many countries, there has been definite progress in effecting necessary measures. Such progress to date, many would agree, is indeed a great achievement in such a short period, and is not often seen. Those of us with experience in policy making should not underestimate the strenuous efforts and determined will that have been shown by our fellow monetary officials in Eastern Europe and the USSR in bringing these measures into effect.

Looking back to last year, when a conference was held by the Federal Reserve Bank of Kansas City on "Central Banking Issues in Emerging Market Economies," the gravest concern then was on issues relating to the banking framework, including the need for the two-tier banking system, the fundamental role of a central bank. A year later, it seems that the major issues of financial reform in Eastern Europe and the USSR have widened from building a framework to finding ways to provide concrete substance to the newly emerging legislative structures. But, of course, I would not deny that issues discussed last year remain important, as in other parts of the world. Among others, establishing the credibility of a financial system and examining the desirable relationship between a government and a central bank are, and will continue to be, important practical issues.

Tadaie Yamashita is Deputy Director of the International Department at the Bank of Japan.

The new institutional framework for financial intermediation in the region meets most of the proposals suggested by our colleagues in ministries, central banks, and international institutions in the West. Typically, one element of such proposals, a two-tier banking system, has already become common in the East. Apart from that, most countries represented here have taken steps to introduce financial instruments and create various financial markets, although both are as yet necessarily limited.

As part of programs aimed at giving substance to institutional frameworks, commercial bank units have been increasingly established by domestic capital as well as foreign capital. Moreover, monetary authorities have endeavored to strengthen commercial banks' credit evaluation capabilities and to provide safe and efficient payment systems, aimed at securing the fundamental functions of the financial system as a whole.

Based on the above observations, let me today focus on two areas of concern for the region: first, issues relating to the working of financial intermediaries, in particular banks' credit evaluation capabilities; and, second, ways to establish and secure the credibility of the financial system in the economy.

■ II. The Role of Banks and the Importance of Technical Assistance and a Sound Free Enterprise System

It appears that progress in enhancing the working of financial intermediaries, particularly strengthening banks' credit evaluation capabilities, has so far been rather slow. It has been reported that there are cases in which this has become a serious impediment to the efficient functioning of financial intermediation. One should not disregard the risk that the lack of credit evaluation could become a potential threat to the long-term soundness of the financial system and, moreover, to its stability.

In principle, one of the important advantages of indirect financing is that depositors and borrowers can save the cost of intermediation by delegating to banks the tasks of credit evaluation and the monitoring of borrowers, thereby benefiting from economies of scale and scope that arise from banks' expertise in these respects. The problem that the region is confronted with is that not many banks have such expertise. Since training in internationally acceptable accounting systems and banking practices is essential for credit evaluation, it will likely be some time before banks in this region are able to fulfill the necessary functions expected of them.

Under these circumstances, the question arises as to what will be the major channel for financial intermediation in the interim: securities markets or bank lending.

One has to admit that direct financing through capital markets in the region has certain limitations at this juncture, for two reasons. First, enterprises intending to issue securities, and also market participants evaluating such enterprises, are not accustomed to internationally acceptable accounting systems. For enterprises in the region, it is currently difficult to produce a balance sheet or a profit/loss table comparable to those issued by enterprises in the West. Therefore, it is unlikely that a disclosure of management and performance would be adequate. Second, savings in these countries are not sufficient for the whole economy to absorb a large amount of private securities. Accordingly, it is quite likely that households and corporations will inevitably prefer safer and more liquid assets to private securities until savings have accumulated sufficiently. Therefore, the economies in the region will have to rely on the banking system for the bulk of financial intermediation. Thus, enhancing banks' capabilities is urgently called for.

In this context, and also to prevent a deterioration in banks' management, it is important to provide banks with technical assistance and to strengthen prudential regulations and supervision. Since the monetary authorities in the region have to bear a heavy burden because of the limited number of experienced personnel, we believe that technical assistance from the West could play an indispensable role. In addition, it is expected that the entry of foreign banks into the region will serve to directly transfer expertise and stimulate the region's financial systems by introducing competition. To attract foreign capital, less economic uncertainty and more transparency with respect to investment procedures are desirable.

Some bank functions, for instance, the monitoring of enterprises' activities, the provision of support for medium-term growth of enterprises, and coordination among them, can be provided to a certain extent by other types of institutions, such as consulting firms (as in some East European countries), and trading companies (as in Japan). It seems, however, that since these functions require the effective monitoring of the performance of individual projects and enterprises on the basis of close and established contacts, it is more efficient for banks to assume these tasks.

My arguments so far have dealt only with the financial system. Here, let me touch on the crucial importance that the reform of the real sector has in achieving the desired results in the economy as a whole. I would like to stress that, without substantial reform in the real sector, reform in the financial system per se would bring forth only limited gains. If impediments exist in the real sector, financial intermediaries cannot fulfill their expected role in the efficient allocation of savings.

In this context, it should be emphasized that private initiatives and market forces should be allowed to work without major impediments. In my view, there are at least two critical preconditions necessary for financial reform to generate intended results. First, the liberalization of prices and corporate decisions must be undertaken with maximum effort. If an economy maintains a distorted price structure and restrictions on corporate decisions, financial intermediation may rather augment the degree of distortion. Second, so-called soft budget practices need to be eliminated. Enterprises have to operate on their own market-based decisions and strict financial discipline. It is only in this way that the economies in the region will succeed in avoiding the further accumulation of nonperforming loans and government subsidy payments. The free enterprise system is essential in this respect.

■ III. Establishing the Credibility and Stability of the Financial System

Let me now turn to the issue of how to establish and secure the credibility of the financial system. In my view, there are three main elements: price stability, a safe and efficient payment system, and sound financial intermediaries.

The first element relates to the macroeconomic role of monetary policy. The most important way to acquire financial system credibility is to achieve price stability. It is only with price stability that we can reduce uncertainties regarding the future, thereby securing sustainable economic growth. Moreover, stable prices serve to minimize inequity in income and asset distribution and help stabilize society. Therefore, achieving price stability is the very foundation of the credibility of the financial system.

In the process of establishing credibility, macroeconomic policy could well be linked mechanically to certain formulas in order to avoid discretionary judgements that could occasionally be misunderstood or misused; namely, central banks may choose to impose self-discipline on monetary policy management and announce such disciplinary measures as commitments. Such schemes include the pegging of exchange rates and strict adherence to money supply targets. The former has been adopted by several countries in the region.

In this regard, please allow me to cite from our experience in the rehabilitation period after World War II. In 1949, Japan unified exchange rates and introduced a fixed exchange rate, parallel with a drastic tightening of the fiscal and monetary policy. This package, called the Dodge Line, played the key role in restoring the credibility of the currency and the financial system. Over time, the fixed exchange rate provided economic policy with a somewhat mechanical kind of discipline in the form of a ceiling for the balance-of-payments deficit. In retrospect, one can say that our monetary policy was guided by balance-of-payments developments until the early 1970s. This was probably a typical example of the adjustment mechanism working under the Bretton Woods system.

The second element necessary for the credibility of the financial system is the safety and efficiency of the payment systems. Only where a safe and efficient settlement system is provided can economic transactions be secured. This feature is the basis of both depositors' and borrowers' confidence in the financial system.

The third element is the soundness and stability of the overall financial system. In this regard, banks' self-discipline on the basis of their own decision making as well as supervision by the monetary authorities is essential.

▇ *IV. Conclusion*

In concluding, I would like to say that the monetary authorities in the region have to bear heavy responsibilities under unfavorable circumstances; namely, the authorities have to pursue austere macroeconomic stabilization policies in an environment of slow adjustment on the domestic supply side. In addition, the authorities must enhance financial intermediation with limited expertise. To minimize possible distortion and to facilitate the smooth functioning of the financial system under these circumstances, it is necessary to accelerate the pace of structural reform in the real sector. To this end, technical assistance will also be useful and effective. And, to save resource costs, stabilization policies based on market mechanisms are most desirable.

Finally, since I am a central banker in Japan, allow me to say a few words on some general lessons that we can derive from our experience some 40 years ago.

As I mentioned earlier, the establishment of the fixed exchange rate system and the implementation of a drastic fiscal consolidation policy in 1949 were the key to regaining credibility of the overall financial system. Among issues relating to the fixed exchange rate system, let me add that a combination of the liberalization of trade account transactions and certain restrictions on capital accounts also importantly helped achieve the efficient functioning of the fixed exchange rate system. In addition, the large-scale rationing of credit and production materials (the so-called *keisha seisan* scheme), which was in effect for a few years after the end of World War II, fulfilled its intended role—namely, it contributed to securing absolute minimum production for Japan's economy, which was then in great turmoil.

However, it appears to me that there are several points to note when applying our past experience. One is crisis management versus more permanent measures. A second is the degree of competition and exposure to markets. A third is the degree of expectation of short-term gains from reform among the population.

For instance, in evaluating the rationing of credit and production resources in the postwar period, one has to recognize that it was effective as a crisis management tool, and that we did not intend to make it permanent. I do not deny that there were items subject to administrative guidance for a longer period, but I have to say that this was mostly to avoid excessive competition and major market failures. This is in sharp contrast to inadequate competition in countries currently in transition, which need to increase competition.

The existence of a competitive environment is also the key to the effectiveness of a fixed exchange rate system. In this regard, we should not ignore the risk that, in the economies of Eastern Europe and the USSR, without adequate competition and flexible responses on the supply side, the effectiveness of fixed exchange rate systems might be eroded, resulting only in frequent rate adjustments.

In considering the role of specialized banks for long-term finance in Japan, which were introduced in the 1950s, one needs to take account of the fact that the following conditions existed for their successful contribution to economic growth in the 1950s and 1960s: namely, adequate competition in the economy, past exposure of banks and enterprises to markets, and expertise that had been acquired by the bank staff. These conditions have been stressed by the former management of these banks as the basis for efficient performance.

It is reported that there are high expectations of a short-term economic recovery in Eastern Europe and the USSR. However, the long absence of a market economy and such high expectations among society could be a handicap for the conduct of economic policy and structural reform.

In sum, a consideration of these points tells us that the countries in the region are faced with greater difficulties than Western Europe and Japan were in the postwar period. This strongly suggests that those who are inside the region and outside need to have much more patience in evaluating the results produced by the reform efforts.

Report on the Conference on "Money, Banking and Credit in Eastern Europe and the Soviet Union," May 15–18, 1991, Tokyo

"Money, Banking & Credit in Eastern Europe and the Soviet Union" was the subject of the first conference held in Tokyo, Japan, by the Institute for East-West Security Studies. The purpose of the meeting was to bring the practitioners in the reforming banking and finance sectors of Eastern Europe and the Soviet Union together with Western experts. Conference participants heard reports on the status of banking reforms in Poland, Hungary, the Czech and Slovak Federal Republic, the Soviet Union, Bulgaria, and Romania. In response, bankers and finance experts from Japan, the United States, and Western Europe offered their analyses of the progress made so far and the relative merits of impending reform steps and sequences.

David M. Kemme, the Institute's Pew Economics Scholar-in-Residence, chaired the conference, which was organized with the valuable assistance of the Mitsui Marine Research Institute and the Japan Center for International Finance and held at the Imperial Hotel, Tokyo, from May 15 to 18, 1991.

The Macroeconomic Setting for Banking Reform in Eastern Europe and the Soviet Union

All the countries in the region face macroeconomic difficulties. Inflation is the first concern in all these economies, due to rising energy prices, reduction or elimination of subsidies, and decontrol of prices. In several countries, inflation appears to have leveled off within several months of price liberalization. Czechoslovakia, for example, reported that prices rose 25.8% in January, the month prices were decontrolled, then rose 7% in February, 4.7% in March, and appeared to have reached a stable level in April. Bulgaria saw a similar phenomenon after prices were liberalized in February. Poland's current inflation level was reported at 55% for the first five months of 1991 on an annualized basis, but the monthly rate is progressively falling.

Budget deficits, growing unemployment (though still at relatively low levels), and declining industrial output also characterize most of the transition economies. Due to the "loss" of the Soviet market and declining exports to other East European countries, these countries also have in common balance of payment problems and shrinking external markets. Convertibility of currencies and issues of internal currency convertibility are key problems that remain to be solved in Bulgaria, Romania, and the Soviet Union. Restrictive monetary policies are the rule. Czechoslovakia and Poland have succeeded over the last year in balancing their government budgets.

Bulgaria was reported to be in a deep economic crisis, with the old economic structure disintegrating and no new structure taking its place. GDP has fallen by 20% in 1991, industrial output declined by 20%–22%, agricultural output by 15%. Meanwhile, Bulgaria's foreign debt is huge: $11.2 billion in 1990; in March 1991, the government announced a moratorium on servicing both principal and interest. Romania's reform was described as "little known, but deep and comprehensive," although the emphasis so far has been on "the preparation of the legal framework."

The Soviet economic situation was characterized as "a period of perestroika, but also of many economic difficulties," including a growing budget deficit, a decline in GNP of 10% and a 10% reduction of industrial output. A three-tier price system is now in effect with fixed prices for "vitally important items, such as staples," regulated prices for other goods, and decontrolled prices for luxury goods. A restructuring of the tax system is also under way.

Progress and Continuing Problems: Toward A Two-Tier Banking System

Throughout the region, the monolithic state banks of the socialist period are being replaced by two-tier banking systems, comprised in each country of a restructured central bank and growing numbers of independent commercial and investment banks. These new banks have begun to function on a genuine business basis, increasingly free from the political manipulations of the past. In Hungary, which began banking reforms in 1987, there are now 37 financial institutions. It was reported that Poland has 50 new banks, nine of them commercial; Czechoslovakia has gone from seven to 30 banks in a year, while Bulgaria now has 70 banks.

The conference found, however, that the numbers of newly created banks do not imply that banking reforms are well advanced. In all these countries a few large banks still dominate the banking business, and the majority of the commercial banks are still state-owned. In Czechoslovakia, for example, two banks continue to control three-quarters of the market. In Bulgaria, the new banks must compete with the 2,500 branches of the enormous State Savings Bank.

Although the reform process appears to be moving rapidly, there are many such barriers to the further development of the new banks and financial systems. Although these difficulties are often similar throughout the region, a remarkable diversity of approaches and priorities has emerged to deal with them. Because each country seems to have its individual mix of concerns and priorities, and is liberalizing at its own chosen pace, conference participants emphasized that the solution must also vary among countries.

In the case of the Soviet Union, the state bank (Gosbank) is being divided into a central bank and commercial banks, including more than 1,380 regional and sector-oriented commercial and cooperative banks. Moreover, Gosbank is developing toward an all-union central bank while republic central banks have already been established in the Russian Federation, Lithuania, Latvia, and Estonia. The potential for rivalry and the likelihood that republic banks would support local interests over those of the union—as has occurred in Yugoslavia—were discussed in detail at the conference. The April 23, 1991 agreement between the Soviet government and ten of the 15 republics would establish a governing council that would determine unified bank policy, including exchange rates, interest rates, and loan standards. It was unclear to the conference participants, however, how secessionist tendencies would affect banking operations and such issues as the financing of the national budget deficit and the establishment of separate currencies by some republics. These problems are unresolved and may be a major stumbling block to the creation of an all-union banking system.

The conference also heard that the Soviet central bank has been greatly modified, has ceased operations with clients, and has become instead a bank for banks, retaining the functions of a note-issuing center and expanding its available instruments for control of monetary policy. It was acknowledged that, despite legal assurances of central bank autonomy, it has been difficult to free bank operations from government interference. Government borrowing to finance the national deficit has had the effect of crowding out individual and enterprise borrowing.

The countries of the region share to varying degrees certain key problems:
1. Banking reform depends on the progress of other economic reforms. The establishment of functioning markets and real prices is still under way.
2. Ownership remains unsettled; most commercial banks are still state-owned.
3. Small, new private institutions must compete with the enormous former state banks, which retain near-monopoly in the banking business.
4. New commercial banks have inherited a large number of bad loans on their balance sheets, which threaten their credibility.
5. Banks continue to operate with varying degrees of government interference, which harms their performance; in Romania and the Soviet Union, for example, despite interest rate "liberalization," the state continues to set interest rates at less than the rate of inflation, making it difficult to attract savings. Confidence in the banks is so low that citizens do not bother to keep their assets in banks.

6. Bank services and management remain far below European and world standards in many areas. The new banks are understaffed, undercapitalized, and have narrow regional or sectoral specializations. They suffer from substandard accounting practices and shortages of other skills and equipment. The new banks lack criteria for granting loans or evaluating the creditworthiness of enterprises seeking loans. Czechoslovak banks, for example, have shown "drastic restraint" in extending credit (injecting only 20 billion korunas into the economy out of 48 billion made available for the purpose of promoting growth) because they have not found enough credible borrowers.
7. Laws to establish and regulate banks are still being passed in the region's parliaments. For example, many countries still lack mortgage laws, commercial courts, and systems to ensure deposits and require bank audits.

The Central Bank: Functions and Autonomy

Conceptions of the role of a central bank—and its difference from a socialist-type national state bank—appeared to vary among the countries in the region. Western conference participants agreed that a central bank must perform three broad functions: 1) conduct monetary policy; 2) oversee the performance of financial markets and banks; and 3) supervise and participate in the operations of the payments system, the means of moving funds from bank to bank and between banks and their customers.

The Western conference participants stressed that if the central bank is to work competently, two other characteristics are key. First, the central bank must operate with complete autonomy, free from the influence of the government: there is accountability, but decision making should be free from political pressures. It was noted that it is inevitable, and perhaps even healthy, that some friction exist between the central bank and the ministry of finance, and that this unfamiliar division should not cause alarm. Second, the central bank should have direct involvement in supervision of commercial banks, particularly to maintain stability throughout the system and to keep problems from spreading. Central bank supervision will play a key role in setting standards and criteria for the new commercial banks, guiding their assessments of the quality of new loans and portfolios according to international standards. This will require trained staff with adequate equipment.

The Role of the Central Bank in Creating Viable Commercial Banks: Clearing Bank Balance Sheets amd Other Issues

Until the present reforms, the East European and Soviet monobanks had no independence and little need or ability to determine the creditworthiness of borrowers. Loans were made according to a plan and were not based upon real economic considerations. The new governments have inherited the consequences of these practices:

low levels of capital and a large number of bad debts that threaten the solvency of the banking systems. New commercial banks in the region must prove themselves to be both solvent and profitable, or they will fail to regain public and international confidence, with their existing capital quickly absorbed by growing loan losses.

With the guidance of the central bank, new banks must establish the integrity of the credit process—the mechanism by which credit is allocated according to the creditworthiness of the borrower. Until the new banks develop procedures to evaluate loans to funnel funds to the most efficient, profitable enterprises, the system will not work overall. Western experience shows that simple recapitalization of banks without the establishment of such a process will only lead to more bad loans. Training will be critical, and Western expertise and assistance can play a vital role in this development.

The establishment of real bank ownership—through shareholding or other forms—is problematic, yet it is vital to the establishment of an effective banking system. Broad-based private ownership by individuals who are interested in the profitability of the bank over the longer run is important for stable, impartial, and efficient management of banking. This will take time to establish, however, and government ownership might be necessary during the interim period; government interests in these new or reconstituted banks can later be sold.

The East European participants argued that at present it is unclear who the shareholders of state-owned banks are and that it is important to move toward private shareholding relatively soon. A problem now exists because the current managers are looking for profits, but are not interested in the value of shares. They are more concerned with getting cash in hand, partly because they do not know how long they will continue to be managers. This has a negative impact on the banks, which should accumulate sufficient cash reserves, but which instead increase salaries and pay out bonuses and dividends. There is therefore a need for "iron rules," which should be provided by the new banking laws. It was noted, however, that shifting to shares alone will not solve the real problems: effective management is also imperative.

Separating the ownership of banks from firms and state enterprises is also key to ensuring the autonomous operation of banking in the future. It is a terrible mistake to allow enterprises to own a large part of a commercial bank from which they are borrowing heavily. The example of Yugoslavia has shown that enterprises with dominant ownership in a bank find it very easy to induce the bank's management to continue extending loans even though the poor performance of the enterprise should limit bank lending. The outcome is the bankruptcy of the bank rather than of the enterprise. The credit process must be independent; this principle is clear from the experience of many countries.

One of the keys to establishing solvent, credible banks is solving the enormous problem of bad debts made in the pre-reform period. There are two approaches: strengthening the capital base of the banks, so that the banks themselves can gradually wipe out the bad debt, as advocated by the Hungarian participants, or the creation of new institutions, the approach being taken by Czechoslovakia. The conference participants were divided on the merits of these approaches.

A typical Western viewpoint was that this should not be seen as a fairness issue. The goal is to minimize the cost. One Western conference participant emphasized that, after all, it would be the taxpayers who would foot the bill for the "bail out" of the banks.

It was emphasized that it is vital to focus on the basic goals of the banks in these countries: to foster savings—because foreign funds for privatization and transition will probably not be sufficiently available—and to provide loans to foster economic development. The new bank system should not be excessively burdened with the old loans. It is more important to develop effective banks, which can then support other types of economic recovery and reform. The solution should be forward-looking—to create credible banks—and should be of minimum cost to the state. It may not be necessary to write off all the debts; some may be recoverable. In the experience of the United States (which also has had some experience with bad debts!), banks are better positioned than government officials to recover a greater percentage of funds from a bad debtor.

The Czechoslovak solution was described in some detail. In March 1991, the Federal Finance Agency created two special "consolidation banks" (one Czech and one Slovak) to serve as "cesspools" where bad loans totalling 100 billion korunas could be concentrated or "dumped." These particular bad loans were "perpetual loans," a form of capital grant or budget subsidy from the old regime, characterized by special low interest rates and no maturity period. Under the new system, they are to be repaid within eight years at an interest rate of 16%— significantly lower than current market rates. Contrary to the policy of normal commercial banks, the state budget will subsidize the interest rate with revenue from long-term savings deposits.

This approach is very controversial, and attempts are being made to force the Finance Ministry to liquidate all of these bad loans quickly, rather than over eight years. After a year, the Ministry will have to explain why it did not liquidate the bad loans, as this 100 billion korunas of perpetual debt may have an inflationary effect. Nothing has been done yet, however, because the consolidation banks now consist only of one general manager and a secretary.

Romania may take a similar approach to that of Czechoslovakia, while Hungary prefers to deal with the bad loans through guarantees by the state, and by spreading them out more or less equally across all commercial banks. These may be covered through income from privatization. The Soviet Union may try to cover the bad debts by increasing the state budget, and also by attempting to recover about half of the debts over time. A large number of Soviet internal debts have already been written off, contributing to the enormous budget deficit problem. In Poland, the real value of bad debts on the books of commercial banks was reduced tremendously by the hyperinflation.

Several emotionally charged issues were raised during the conference, but were not central to the discussions. These included the arguments for and against shock therapy, and the merits of the recent debt reduction to Poland. There was also interesting discussion regarding the relationship between banking reforms and other economic reform policies, and methods to encourage domestic savings.

Applying Solutions From Abroad

Considering the divergence of views on approaches to these problems raised during the conference, there was a surprising amount of interest expressed in mutual learning from the experiences of others. The Western bankers and financial experts offered numerous suggestions based on their own national experiences. Japanese bankers, for example, suggested methods of encouraging savings, of focusing scarce credit and capital to sectors that could best benefit the nation, and of privatizing state-owned enterprises.

Overall, there was a consensus that care must be taken before foreign methods are imported. Some of the East European banking systems are already becoming hybrids: one country reportedly has adopted central bank operations like those of Germany's Bundesbank, a supervisory system from Belgium, commercial banking practices from France, and advisors from the United States. Piecemeal and sometimes contradictory reforms may not fit together over time and run the risk of losing public confidence in the handling of the reform process.

Further Recommendations

In closing, the Western participants offered a number of additional recommendations. First, careful sequencing of reform steps will be vital to the overall success of the reforms. A credible, multi-year program is absolutely vital, so that firms can plan for the future with less uncertainty. Not all activities can move with the same speed; in fact, speed is less important than intelligent sequencing and building confidence. The sequence of reforms should begin with the development of the central bank, followed by the commercial systems, with development of capital and securities markets third. Setting up the banking infrastructure should be done early, as should the restructuring of existing banks—starting with those that can be most easily turned around, so as to demonstrate success quickly and begin to build confidence. Development of accounting standards should also begin early on. A payments system, including technical improvements that promote more efficient transfers, can follow to facilitate the overnight interbank market that will produce more liquidity. Thereafter, a short-term market for government securities will also promote liquidity and show progress in the reform.

Second was the admonition to follow the rule of specificity in reform policies: to avoid mixing several problems together. For example, privatization should be undertaken in order to develop a more efficient system; the goal should not be to gain the revenue that is needed to underwrite another kind of reform. Having more than one objective complicates the intent of the original policy.

Third, as each country undertakes reforms, the international context has to be kept in mind. For example, it was recommended that the East Europeans make efforts to build a banking structure compatible with that of the European Community. It is also very important to acknowledge the increasing international competition for scarce capital; expectations that foreign capital will save the day must be lowered. Each country should make every effort to create attractive environments for foreign investment. Policies should also focus on attracting the domestic sources of savings that exist in at least some of the East European countries—which should increase as confidence grows in the banks and in local currencies.

Although banking reform is far less publicized than price liberalization, privatization, the development of entrepreneurship, and the elements of economic reform, no reform is more important than the reform of the banking and financial system. The conference on "Money, Banking and Credit in Eastern Europe and the Soviet Union" demonstrated the complexity and range of difficulties in this key reform, as well as the variety of approaches and experiments being undertaken across the region.

David Youtz
Rapporteur

List of Participants

*Conference on "Money, Banking and Credit in Eastern Europe
and the Soviet Union"
May 15–18, 1991
Tokyo*

Mr. Junichi Arai
Director of Administration
Mitsui Marine Research Institute
  Co., Ltd.
Japan

Ms. Masako Ayakawa
Senior Economist in the Research
  Department
Industrial Bank of Japan, Ltd.
Japan

Dr. Akos Balassa
Managing Director and Advisor
  to the President
National Bank of Hungary
Hungary

Dr. Alexander Bogomolov
Senior Research Associate &
  Executive Assistant to the
  President
Institute for East-West Security
  Studies
United States

Academician Oleg Bogomolov
Director
Institute for International
  Economic and Political Studies
Academy of Sciences
USSR

Dr. Morris Bornstein
Professor of Economics
University of Michigan
United States

Dr. Katalin Botos
Minister of State
Hungary

Mr. Michio Chano
Director of the European
  Department
Japan Center for International
  Finance
Japan

Mr. Iuri Aleksandrovich Chulkov
Head of the Currency-Financial
  Department
Ministry of Foreign Affairs
USSR

Mr. Vladimir Vladimirovich Esin
Assistant to the Soviet Minister of
  Finance
USSR

Dr. Jacob A. Frenkel
Economic Counsellor and
  Director of Research
International Monetary Fund

Dr. Emil Iota Ghizari
Deputy Governor
National Bank of Romania
Romania

Mr. Kazuyuki Inagawa
Senior Economist
Mitsui Marine Research Institute
  Co, Ltd.
Japan

Mr. Takeru Ishikawa
Chairman
Mitsui Marine and Fire Insurance
  Company
Japan

Dr. Vladimir Jindra
Adviser to the Governor
State Bank of Czechoslovakia
CSFR

Mr. Koji Kakizawa
Member of the House of
  Representatives of the
  National Diet
Japan

Mr. Takatoshi Kato
Deputy Director-General
International Finance Bureau
Ministry of Finance
Japan

Dr. David M. Kemme
Pew Economics Scholar-in-
  Residence
Institute for East-West Security
  Studies
United States

Mr. Igor A. Kniazev
Senior Economist
State Bank of the USSR
USSR

Ms. Harumi Kuroda
Administrative Assistant
Mitsui Marine Research Institute
  Co., Ltd.
Japan

Mr. Rei Masunaga
Deputy President
Japan Center for International
  Finance
Japan

Mr. Yasuo Matsushita
Chairman
Mitsui-Taiyo-Kobe Bank
Japan

Dr. Mileti Mladenov
Deputy Governor
Bulgarian National Bank
Bulgaria

Ms. Satomi Murai
Senior Economist in the Research
  Department
Industrial Bank of Japan
Japan

Dr. Sadoa Nagaoka
Director
Soviet Union and Eastern
  European Office
Ministry of International Trade
  and Industry
Japan

Mr. Taro Nakayama
Minister of Foreign Affairs
Japan

Mr. John Neuffer
Senior Research Fellow
Mitsui Marine Research Institute
  Co., Ltd.
Japan

Mr. Takekazu Okita
Economist
Mitsui Marine Research Institute
  Co., Ltd.
Japan

H.E. Vladimir Efimovich Orlov
Minister of Finance
USSR

Ambassador Hisashi Owada
Deputy Minister of Foreign
  Affairs
Japan

Dr. J. Andrew Spindler
Senior Vice President
Federal Reserve Bank
United States

Dr. Gunter Storch
Member of the Board
Deutsche Bundesbank
Federal Republic of Germany

Mr. Shigemitsu Sugisaki
Deputy Minister of Finance for
  International Affairs
Japan

Mr. Wieslaw Szczuka
First Secretary
Embassy of Poland
Japan

Ms. Miyuki Takata
Administrative Assistant
Mitsui Marine Research Institute
  Co., Ltd.
Japan

Mr. Kiyoshi Teramoto
Adviser to the Governor of the
  Bank of Japan
Japan

Mr. Ichiro Uchida
Senior Adviser to the President
Mitsui Marine and Fire Insurance
  Company, Ltd.
Japan

Mr. Michio Watanabe
Member of the House of
  Representatives of the
  National Diet
Japan

Dr. Norbert Wieczorek
Member of the Bundestag
Federal Republic of Germany

Mr. Keith Wind
Director of Conferences and
  Special Projects
Institute for East-West Security
  Studies
United States

Mr. Tadaie Yamashita
Deputy Director
International Department
Bank of Japan
Japan

Mr. Hiroyoshi Yamazaki
Japan Center for International
  Finance
Japan

Mr. Makoto Yoshie
Senior Managing Director
Mitsui-Taiyo-Kobe Bank
Japan

Mr. Kazuo Yoshimura
Senior Economist
Industrial Bank of Japan
Japan

Mr. David Youtz
Research Associate and
  Coordinator of Asian Programs
Institute for East-West Security
  Studies
United States

Dr. Vyacheslav S. Zakharov
Deputy Chairman of the Board
State Bank of the USSR
USSR

ABOUT THE EDITORS

David M. Kemme, the former Pew Economics Scholar-in-Residence at the Institute for East-West Security Studies in New York, is now the W. Frank Barton Faculty Fellow at the Wichita State University in Kansas. He was a Fulbright Lecturer at the Main School of Planning and Statistics in Warsaw (1981–1982), and has researched and published extensively on productivity and efficiency in Eastern Europe and the Soviet Union, disequilibrium macroeconomics, and the chronic shortage model of centrally planned economies. Dr. Kemme has published widely in such journals as *Soviet Studies, Journal of Comparative Economics*, and *Economic Systems* and most recently has authored *Economic Transition in Eastern Europe and the Soviet Union: Issues and Strategies*, IEWSS Occasional Paper Series, no. 20 (New York, 1991); he is also the editor of *Economic Reform in Poland* (Greenwich, CT: JAI Press, 1991) and *Technology Markets and Export Controls in the 1990s* (New York: New York University, 1991). In addition, Dr. Kemme is North American Editor of *Economics of Planning*.

Andrzej Rudka is Senior Research Fellow at the Institute for East-West Security Studies in New York. In 1990–1991 he was Senior Fulbright Scholar in the Department of Economics at George Washington University, Washington, DC. In 1989 and 1991 he was a Visiting Professor at the College of Saint Rose in Albany, New York. Dr. Rudka served as Deputy Director and Senior Research Fellow at the Foreign Trade Research Institute in Warsaw, and was a member of the Working Group on Medium-Term Prospects and Structural Changes in the World Economy of the European Association of Business Cycle Institutes. Dr. Rudka has written on East-West trade, technology transfer and export controls, Polish-US economic relations, the US and the world economy, and Polish foreign trade. His most recent work is "Western Export Controls: An East European View," in *Technology Markets and Export Controls in the 1990s*, ed. David M. Kemme (New York: New York University, 1991).